Editors

Richard A. Villa & Jacqueline S. Thousand

Creating an Inclusive School

2nd edition

Association for Supervision and Curriculum Development • Alexandria, Virginia USA

P9-CNH-038

Association for Supervision and Curriculum Development
1703 N. Beauregard St. • Alexandria, VA 22311-1714 USA
Telephone: 800-933-2723 or 703-578-9600 • Fax: 703-575-5400
Web site: http://www.ascd.org • E-mail: member@ascd.org

Gene R. Carter, *Executive Director;* Nancy Modrak, *Director of Publishing;* Julie Houtz, *Director of Book Editing & Production;* Deborah Siegel, *Project Manager;* Georgia Park, *Senior Graphic Designer;* Jim Beals, *Typesetter;* Tracey A. Franklin, *Production Manager.*

Printed in the United States of America. Cover art copyright © 2005 by ASCD.

ASCD publications present a variety of viewpoints. The views expressed or implied in this book should not be interpreted as official positions of the Association.

All Web links in this book are correct as of the publication date below but may have become inactive or otherwise modified since that time. If you notice a deactivated or changed link, please e-mail books@ascd.org with the words "Link Update" in the subject line. In your message, please specify the Web link, the book title, and the page number on which the link appears.

ASCD Member Book, No. FY05-05 (February 2005, P). ASCD Member Books mail to Premium (P), Comprehensive (C), and Regular (R) members on this schedule: Jan., PC; Feb., P; Apr., PCR; May, P; July, PC; Aug., P; Sept., PCR; Nov., PC; Dec., P

Paperback ISBN: 1-4166-0049-3 • ASCD product #105019 • List Price: $26.95 ($20.95 ASCD member price, direct from ASCD only)

e-books ($26.95): Retail PDF ISBN 1-4166-0212-7 • netLibrary ISBN 1-4166-0210-0 • ebrary ISBN 1-4166-0211-9

Library of Congress Cataloging-in-Publication Data

Creating an inclusive school / Richard A. Villa and Jacqueline S. Thousand, editors.— 2nd ed.
       p. cm.
   Includes bibliographical references and index.
   ISBN 1-4166-0049-3 (alk. paper)
   1. Children with disabilities—Education—United States. 2. Mainstreaming in education—United States. 3. School management and organization—United States. I. Villa, Richard A., 1952- II. Thousand, Jacqueline S., 1950-

   LC4031.C74 2005
   371.9'046—dc22

                           2004023185

10 09 08 07 06 05   12 11 10 9 8 7 6 5 4 3 2 1

Creating an Inclusive School

2nd Edition

Preface

Richard A. Villa and Jacqueline S. Thousand

In 1975, Congress passed the Education for All Handicapped Children Act (Public Law 94–142) guaranteeing for the first time that all students with disabilities would receive a public education. The law's name was changed in a subsequent reauthorization in 1990 to the Individuals with Disabilities Education Act (IDEA). The law provides the foundation for inclusive schooling, requiring that every child with a disability receive a free and appropriate public education and learn in the least restrictive environment.

At the time the first edition of this book was written, discussions on inclusion provoked strong and differing opinions among educators. Since that time, research, experience, and case law have further clarified the rights and responsibilities of school personnel to include students with disabilities with nondisabled peers in general education settings to the maximum extent appropriate and have documented the benefits of inclusive education for students with and without disabilities. The percentage of students with disabilities within general education environments continues to increase, and we can expect this trend to continue.

The 1997 reauthorization of IDEA, which occurred two years after the publication of the first edition of this book, greatly strengthened the presumption that the placement of first choice for students with disabilities should be in the general education environment where they most readily would have access to the rigorous general education curriculum as well as other noncurricular activities to which other classmates had access. The 2001 No Child Left Behind (NCLB) Act has also bolstered public expectations that schools foster and be held accountable for high educational standards, better instruction and learning, equality of opportunity to learn, and excellence in student performance for all students with and without disabilities. A promising NCLB requirement is for all teachers to meet the standards that would certify them as highly qualified in every subject area they teach. Historically, special educators have been responsible for teaching the core subjects (i.e., language arts, social studies, science, mathematics) to special education–eligible students in separate classrooms. With NCLB, these educators, particularly those at the middle and secondary level, no longer would be able to do this without certification in each subject area taught. However, if they and their special education–eligible students join general education classes by coteaching and planning with highly qualified content-area general educators, all students not only access highly qualified instructors but also enjoy the complementary skills of special educators proficient in differentiating instruction for any student in the classroom. Coteaching and the collaborative planning that accompanies it are not only practical solutions to the certification dilemma NCLB creates for special educators but also powerful organizational and instructional approaches that have the potential of advancing inclusive education even further by promoting the union of general and special educators for the benefit of all students.

We have written a second edition for several reasons. First, almost 30 years after the law came into effect, many educators still do not understand IDEA or how to implement it. Second, although schools and districts across the country have been educating students with disabilities in inclusive settings for many years, there still remain schools that have a long way to go toward implementing the spirit and the letter of this law. Families often have to fight to get their children into general education classrooms and inclusive settings. Third, some school personnel believe they are implementing inclusive practices when in fact they are not. A student's physical presence in general education does not constitute the academic and social integration that is a hallmark of quality inclusive education. In other words, we still have bad examples of a good practice—

inclusion. A fourth reason is that the proactive universal design approach to lesson and unit planning has replaced the after-the-fact, retrofit approach of developing accommodations and modifications for select students. This is a dramatic shift in thinking in education and one that is examined carefully in this second edition. The final reason we decided to write a second edition is because the field of education has evolved over the past decade; we now have greater knowledge and evidence of the success of various organizational and instructional practices that support the education of students with and without disabilities in shared environments.

Contributors to this second edition have been heavily involved in and are very knowledgeable about the evolution of inclusive educational practices. Thus they are able to offer readers the legal and historical background of inclusive education, a constellation of rationales for inclusion, advice on how to facilitate the transformation of schools so as to embrace an inclusive ethic and practice, promising educational practices supportive of differentiating instruction for diverse learners, and answers to common questions and concerns about inclusive education. Throughout the book, you will discover moving and compelling "Voices of Inclusion" written by teachers, administrators, and parents of students with disabilities.

We hope that you will find this book a valuable addition to your professional library and that it will assist you in creating and advancing school cultures that welcome, value, empower, and support the diverse academic and social learning of all students in shared environments and experiences.

●　●　●　●　●

Chapter 1

What Is an Inclusive School?

Mary A. Falvey and Christine C. Givner

There is only one child in the world and that child's name is ALL children.

—Carl Sandburg

An Inclusive Classroom in Action

What does an inclusive school look and sound like? The following scenario describes a typical day in freshman language arts class for 32 students attending an ordinary, yet extraordinary, high school in a large urban school district.

The students in Mr. Rice's third period have just finished "reading" the final chapter of *To Kill a Mockingbird* by Harper Lee (1960). Some students have listened to the book on tape because of their literacy levels, while other students were given (or created for themselves) graphic organizers to help them organize key ideas. The students have been working on 9th grade California literacy standards while reading the book. Although these students are diverse in their learning styles and abilities, all are challenged in meaningful ways that relate to the 9th grade standards. Mr. Rice has just assigned a culminating task that asks the students to creatively depict how the characters in *To Kill a Mockingbird* demonstrated courage and conviction. He also has distributed a rubric describing how the assignments will be evaluated.

Several students in Mr. Rice's class qualify for special education; five qualify for gifted and talented services. In collaboration with Mr. Rice, the coordinator of the gifted and talented support services, Ms. Stremel, has contracted with each of those five students about how they will not only meet but also exceed the assignment rubric. Mr. Rice and Ms. Stremel are available at any time to assist and guide the five students as they complete their modified assignments and to help other students with their assignments. Ms. Mikel, Mr. Rice's special education support teacher, is also in the classroom and is available to help students eligible for special education and anyone else who seeks assistance.

Jesús, one of Mr. Rice's third period students, qualifies for special education services because of a learning disability. He reads well below grade level but has excellent verbal and visual/spatial skills. For the assignment, Jesús is partnered with Emily, who has high reading and writing skills but struggles with verbal skills. The two students use their complementary strengths to put together a joint presentation on how the *To Kill a Mockingbird* characters demonstrated courage and conviction.

George, a student with autism, and Quon receive guidance in designing their presentation. George will show pictures of the characters with brief written descriptions that he and Quon have composed. Lonny, a socially talented senior, is completing his community service requirements by supporting George and the other students in this third period class.

Casandra, who has multiple disabilities, uses an electric wheelchair to get around and an electronic communication aid to convey her thoughts and responses. Casandra's partner is Jimmy, a classmate who qualifies for gifted and talented services. Jimmy surfs the Web for information related to the topic and then decides with Casandra what to include in their presentation. Casandra and Jimmy enter their content into Casandra's electronic communication device, which has a voice output that will be activated to deliver their presentation in class.

Two students are English-language learners. One student speaks Cantonese, and the other speaks Spanish. Each is partnered with a bilingual classmate. The two pairs of students prepare

2

bilingual presentations in their languages: one pair in Cantonese and English and the other pair in Spanish and English. All visual aids are also presented in both languages.

The composition of Mr. Rice's class reflects the diversity in most classrooms in the United States. At one time, many students in such a class would have been labeled and forced into separate classes, thereby limiting their exposure to one another, the essential curriculum, and varied instructional procedures and personnel. Some students would have been moved to a gifted and talented program. Jesús, Casandra, and George would have been classified as disabled and placed in a segregated special education program. The students speaking languages other than English would have been placed in a separate bilingual or English-as-a-second-language program, where they would have limited exposure to English-speaking peers. *a drawback*

Some people argue that the social justice occurring in Mr. Rice's class—inclusive education—is not the responsibility of schools. However, if inclusive education is not the schools' responsibility, then whose is it? Our country's systems and institutions teach by example what a country, state, or community values: either inclusion, or segregation and exclusion. Inclusive education demands that schools create and provide whatever is necessary to ensure that all students have access to meaningful learning. It does not require students to possess any particular set of skills or abilities as a prerequisite to belonging.

Y'ure either for or against inclusion.

Inclusive Education: Legal Definition

The legal mandate driving inclusive education in the United States is Public Law (P.L.) 94–142, now the Individuals with Disabilities Education Act (IDEA). Although the specific terms *inclusion* and *inclusive education* cannot be found in P.L. 94–142, the definition of *least restrictive environment* (LRE) is a key element of the law. It provided the initial legal impetus for creating inclusive education. The law states that

> to the maximum extent appropriate, handicapped children,
> including those children in public and private institutions or

other care facilities, are educated with children who are not handicapped, and that special classes, separate schooling, or other removal of handicapped children from the regular educational environment occurs only when the nature or severity of the handicap is such that education in regular classes with the use of supplementary aids and services cannot be achieved satisfactorily. (P.L. 94–142, § 1412 [5] [B])

The critical language used in the law is "with the use of supplementary aids and services." In 1975, when P.L. 94–142 was passed, the professional education literature was devoid of any information on and strategies for using supplementary aids and services to effectively include students with disabilities. However, since that time, the use of such aids and services to include all students has been frequently identified and described in the literature. (Some recent examples include Falvey, 1996; Fisher, Sax, & Pumpian, 1999; Janney & Snell, 2000; Kennedy & Fisher, 2001; Thousand, Villa, & Nevin, 2002; Villa & Thousand, 2000.) As a result, the LRE mandate has been a leading force in the design and implementation of inclusive education.

Since the promulgation of IDEA (P.L. 94–142) the federal court decisions have built on one another to clarify the following:

- School districts must consider placement in general education for all students with disabilities, regardless of the degree of the disability.
- Academic and social benefits of placement in general education must be taken into consideration.
- Such consideration must be more than a token gesture.
- Placement in the LRE is not "dumping" but rather placing students with disabilities in general education settings with the necessary supports, services, and supplementary aids.

The standard for denying inclusive education to a student with disabilities is very high.

Inclusive Education: Pragmatic Definition

What is inclusion, or inclusive education? To begin to answer that question, we asked thousands of children, adolescents, and adults to identify an event in their lives that caused them to feel included and one that caused them to feel excluded. We also asked the subjects to describe how they felt during and following the two experiences. Figure 1.1 provides a sampling of the feelings that people have reported experiencing when they felt included or excluded.

Examining such reactions is a critical element in a book about educating all students. Figure 1.1 makes the powerful point that no one wants to be excluded. Inclusive education is about embracing everyone and making a commitment to provide each student in the community, each citizen in a democracy, with the inalienable right to belong. Inclusion assumes that living and learning together benefits everyone, not just children who are labeled as having a difference (e.g., those who are gifted, are non–English proficient, or have a disability).

In summary, inclusion is a belief system, not just a set of strategies. Mr. Rice's language arts class is not just about accommodations and supports; it is about an attitude and a disposition that a school intentionally teaches by example. Once adopted by a school or school district, an inclusive vision drives all decisions and actions by those who subscribe to it. People no longer ask, "Why inclusion?" They ask, "How do we successfully include all students?"

Inclusive Education Implications

Inclusion, as Figure 1.1 illustrates, is the opposite of segregation and isolation. Segregated education creates a permanent underclass of students and conveys a strong message to those students that they do not measure up, fit in, or belong. Segregationist thinking assumes that the right to belong is an earned rather than an unconditional human right. Norman Kunc (2000) speaks of the casualties of exclusion, or "conditional acceptance." He suggests that many of the current problems facing children and youth at risk (e.g., gangs, suicide, and dropping out of school) are the casualties of an inflexible,

Figure 1.1

Responses to the questions, "How did you feel when you were . . ."

EXCLUDED?	INCLUDED?
• angry	• proud
• resentful	• secure
• hurt	• special
• frustrated	• comfortable
• lonely	• recognized
• different	• confident
• confused	• happy
• isolated	• excited
• inferior	• trusted
• worthless	• cared about
• invisible	• liked
• substandard	• accepted
• unwanted	• appreciated
• untrusted	• reinforced
• unaccepted	• loved
• closed	• grateful
• ashamed	• normal
	• open
	• positive
	• nurtured
	• important
	• responsible
	• grown up

insensitive system of education that systematically (although perhaps unintentionally) destroys the self-esteem and self-worth of students who do not "fit the mold." In a seminal work that describes the plight of youth at risk from a Native American perspective, Brendtro, Brokenleg, and Van Bockern (2002) describe *belonging* as one of the four central values that create a child's *Circle of Courage*. The right to belong is every person's birthright. Given the increasing numbers of at-risk students in U.S. schools and the centrality of the need to belong, schools must provide a way to reclaim youth labeled at risk, disabled, homeless, gay or lesbian, and so forth.

The growing diversity of the student population in U.S. schools is a topic of great debate and concern. Differences among students may include language, culture, religion, gender, varied abilities, sexual preference, socioeconomic status, and geographic setting. The differences are often spoken about as a problem rather than an opportunity for learning what rich variety exists in others' lives and how we can be included, valued, respected, and welcomed for who we are in a naturally diverse world. In 1992, Grant Wiggins wrote the following about the value of diversity:

> We will not successfully restructure schools to be effective until we stop seeing diversity in students *as a problem*. Our challenge is not one of getting "special" students to better adjust to the usual schoolwork, the usual teacher pace, or the usual tests. The challenge of schooling remains what it has been since the modern era began two centuries ago: ensuring that *all* students receive their entitlement. They have the *right* to thought-provoking and enabling schoolwork, so that they might use their minds well and discover the joy therein to willingly push themselves farther. They have the *right* to instruction that obligates the teacher, like the doctor, to change tactics when progress fails to occur. They have the *right* to assessment that provides students and teachers with insight into real-world standards, useable feedback, the opportunity to self-assess, and the chance to have dialogue with, or even to challenge, the assessor—also a *right* in a democratic culture. Until such a time, we will have no insight into human potential. Until the challenge is met, schools will continue to reward the lucky or the already-equipped and weed out the poor performers. (pp. xv–xvi)

Inclusive Education: School Restructuring

The call for restructuring of American education to establish meaningful educational standards (i.e., student outcomes) and to hold schools accountable for accomplishing those outcomes with every student requires great individual and collective commitment and effort. All restructuring efforts in schools require, at the minimum, a belief that

- Each student can and will learn and succeed.
- Diversity enriches us all, and students at risk can overcome the risk for failure through involvement in a thoughtful and caring community of learners.
- Each student has unique contributions to offer to other learners.
- Each student has strengths and needs.
- Services and supports should not be relegated to one setting (e.g., special classes or schools).
- Effective learning results from the collaborative efforts of everyone working to ensure each student's success.

Systems change initiatives in special education are paralleling systems change efforts in general education. Such initiatives for change are often referred to as school restructuring. Fundamental questions regarding the most effective strategies for teaching all students are being raised, and numerous innovative and highly effective strategies are being designed and implemented. School restructuring efforts are described in greater detail in Chapters 4–6 and are summarized below:

- Heterogeneous and cooperative group arrangements of students are used because they are more effective for learning (Johnson & Johnson, 2002; Oakes, 1985; Oakes & Lipton, 2003; Sapon-Shevin, 1994).
- Students are provided with individualized approaches to curriculum, assessment (e.g., nonbiased assessment

procedures, multiple approaches to intelligence—see Carr
& Harris, 2001; Hock, 2000), and instruction because of
high expectations held for all students (Castellano, 2003).
- Staff, students, parents, and community members collaborate in the design and delivery of effective education for
all students (Thousand, Villa, & Nevin, 2002; Villa & Thousand, 2000).
- Teachers and other professionals are giving students the
opportunity to learn to think and be creative, and not just to
repeat information that they have memorized (Kohn, 1999;
Lenz & Schumaker, 1999; Schumm, 1999; Tomlinson, 1999).
- School staff members are facilitating students' social skills
as students interact, relate to one another, and develop relationships and friendships (Delpit, 1995; Noddings, 1992).

As the characteristics of the school restructuring movement take
hold in more and more schools, inclusion of students with disabilities does not become a separate and distinct action; instead, it
occurs simultaneously and naturally. The characteristics of both the
school restructuring movement and the building of inclusive
schools are the same: all students must experience quality education that meets their specific educational needs in the context of
political and social justice.

Summary

We have offered a number of ways to define inclusive schools. We do
not subscribe to any one definition. However, we believe that we
must create, cherish, and nurture schools that include and effectively educate all students.

Inclusion benefits not only students with disabilities, but also
all students, educators, parents, and community members. Experience tells us that as communities and schools embrace the true
meaning of inclusion, they become better able to change a segregated special education system into an inclusive service delivery
system and to change a society and world intolerant and fearful of

difference into one that embraces and celebrates natural diversity with meaningful, student-centered learning.

Even after inclusion is operationally defined, it remains an elusive term. Part of the confusion arises from assumptions associated with inclusion—that it is a program or that it is a research-devised strategy. The underlying assumption, however, is that inclusion is a way of life—a way of living together—that is based on a belief that each individual is valued and belongs.

References

Brendtro, L. K., Brokenleg, M., & Van Bockern, S. L. (2002). *Reclaiming youth at risk: Our hope for the future* (Rev. ed.). Bloomington, IN: National Educational Service.

Carr, J. F., & Harris, D. E. (2001). *Succeeding with standards: Linking curriculum, assessment, and action planning.* Alexandria, VA: Association for Supervision and Curriculum Development.

Castellano, J. (2003). *Special populations in gifted education: Working with diverse gifted learners.* Boston: Allyn and Bacon.

Delpit, L. (1995). *Other people's children: Cultural conflict in the classroom.* New York: New Press.

Falvey, M. (Ed.).(1995). *Inclusive and heterogeneous schooling: Assessment, curriculum, and instruction.* Baltimore: Paul H. Brookes.

Fisher, D., Sax, C., & Pumpian, I. (Eds.). (1999). *Inclusive high schools: Learning from contemporary classrooms.* Baltimore: Paul H. Brookes.

Hock, M. (2000). Standards, assessment, and Individualized Education Programs. In R. A. Villa & J. S. Thousand (Eds.), *Restructuring for caring and effective education: Piecing the puzzle together* (2nd ed., pp. 208–241). Baltimore: Paul H. Brookes.

Individuals with Disabilities Education Act (IDEA) Amendments of 1997, P.L. 105–117, 20 U.S.C. §§ 1400 *et seq.*

Janney, R., & Snell, M. E. (2000). *Modifying schoolwork.* Baltimore: Paul H. Brookes.

Johnson, D. W., & Johnson, R. (2002). Cooperative community, constructive conflict, and civic values. In J. S. Thousand, R. A. Villa, & A. I. Nevin (Eds.), *Creativity and collaborative learning: The practical guide to empowering students, teachers, and families* (2nd ed., pp. 181–196). Baltimore: Paul H. Brookes.

Kennedy, C. H., & Fisher, D. (2001). *Inclusive middle schools.* Baltimore: Paul H. Brookes.

Kohn, A. (1999). *The schools our children deserve: Moving beyond traditional classrooms and "tougher standards."* Boston: Houghton Mifflin.

Kunc, N. (2000). Rediscovering the right to belong. In R. A. Villa & J. S. Thousand (Eds.), *Restructuring for caring and effective education: Piecing the puzzle together* (2nd ed. pp. 77–92). Baltimore: Paul H. Brookes.

Lee, H. (1960). *To kill a mockingbird*. Philadelphia: Lippincott.

Noddings, N. (1992). *The challenge to care in schools: An alternative approach to education*. New York: Teachers College Press.

Oakes, J. (1985). *Keeping track: How schools structure inequality*. New Haven, CT: Yale University Press.

Oakes, J., & Lipton, M. (2003). *Teaching to change the world* (2nd ed.). Boston: McGraw-Hill.

Sapon-Shevin, M. (1994). *Playing favorites: Gifted education and the disruption of community*. Albany, NY: State University of New York Press.

Schumaker, J. & Lenz, K., (1999). *Adapting language arts, social studies, and science materials for the inclusive classroom*. Reston, VA: Council for Exceptional Children.

Schumm, J. S. (1999). *Adapting reading and math materials for the inclusive classroom*. Reston, VA: Council for Exceptional Children.

Thousand, J. S., Villa, R. A., & Nevin, A. I. (Eds.). (2002). *Creativity and collaborative learning: The practical guide to empowering students, teachers, and families* (2nd ed.). Baltimore: Paul H. Brookes.

Tomlinson, C. A. (1999). *The differentiated classroom: Responding to the needs of all learners*. Alexandria, VA: Association for Supervision and Curriculum Development.

Villa, R. A., & Thousand, J. S. (2000). Restructuring public school systems: Strategies for organizational change and progress. In R. A. Villa & J. S. Thousand (Eds.), *Restructuring for caring and effective education: Piecing the puzzle together* (2nd ed., pp. 7–37). Baltimore: Paul H. Brookes.

Wiggins, G. (1992). Foreward. In R. A. Villa, J. S. Thousand, W. Stainback, & S. Stainback (Eds.), *Restructuring for caring and effective education: An administrative guide to creating heterogeneous schools* (pp. xv–xvi). Baltimore: Paul H. Brookes.

Chapter 2

Inclusive Education: Historical Perspective

Susan Bray Stainback and Julie Smith

"For practically all of the history of civilization, education has been for the elite, and educational practices have reflected an elitist orientation" (Blankenship & Lilly, 1981, p. 18). Until approximately 1800 in the United States, most students with disabilities were not deemed worthy of education at all. Throughout the 19th century and much of the 20th, when children with disabilities received an education, it was institutionalized and segregated. Recent years have witnessed a movement—sometimes slow and hesitant, but always progressive— toward inclusive education for many previously segregated learners. Now, as we progress through the 21st century, the goal of universal inclusive education is potentially within our grasp, although progress has been hard won. This chapter reviews the path climbed toward inclusion in U.S. schools.

Early Years of Education

For most U.S. students who were considered poor or minority or who were diagnosed with a disability, the first hurdle was merely to receive an education. For example, the first state-supported plan proposed by Thomas Jefferson in 1779 to provide the poor of Virginia with an education was rejected "by the refusal of well-to-do citizens to pay taxes for the education of the poor" (Sigmon, 1983, p. 5). Approximately one century after Jefferson's proposal, the efforts of educational leaders such as Horace Mann, coupled with the massive influx of immigrants during the late 1800s and early 1900s who were perceived by the populace as needing to be "Americanized," persuaded affluent Americans that education of the "lower" classes was in the best interest of the country. As a result, publicly supported education was adopted, and all states passed compulsory education attendance laws between 1842 and 1918.

Not all developments were positive, however. The "separate but equal" mandate, conceived in Massachusetts in 1850 and nationally adopted by the Supreme Court in 1896, provided the impetus to condone segregation in the schools (Fonder & Kennedy, 2004). When members of racial minority groups, immigrants, and indigenous Americans were educated, their education occurred in a separate system or on lower, nonacademic tracks (Hooks, 2000). Finally, although school attendance was compulsory, exceptions were made for early school exit. As a result, some children from lower socioeconomic groups left school early to enter the workforce. Those financial necessities and realities worked against achieving a truly integrated education for all students.

Education for Students with Disabilities

In the late 1700s, the physician Benjamin Rush introduced the concept of educating people with disabilities. It was not until 1817, however, that the first educational program for individuals with disabilities was established by Thomas Gallaudet at the American Asylum for the Education and Instruction of the Deaf and Dumb in Connecticut. Other programs for educating students who had various disabilities soon followed. By the early 1900s, nearly every state had built institutions for people considered blind, deaf, or "mentally retarded." People with physical disabilities were often thought to be mentally retarded and were also confined in such institutions (Anderson, 1998). Most children with disabilities—whether living in institutions or at home—did not receive an education at the time. Those who did often received their schooling in asylums or in government- or church-supported institutions. Sigmon (1983, p. 3) notes that "almost all children who were wheelchair-bound, not toilet trained, or considered uneducable were excluded because of the problems that schooling them would entail." A movement to establish special classes for such children who were allowed to attend school resulted in their exclusion from general education classes. "Special classes came about, not for humanitarian reasons but because such children were unwanted in the regular public school classroom. Feelings against . . . placing them in regular classrooms were strong" (Chaves, 1977, p. 30). Of course, we do not mean to imply that individuals who worked in special classes and special education have had anything but humanitarian motives. Ainscow (1991) noted the paradox of special educators. While attempting to meet the educational needs of students, the "special" learning settings generally limited natural critical learning opportunities.

Special classes and special day schools gathered momentum in the early 1900s, although educational programs in asylums and residential institutions for students with disabilities continued to expand (Racino, 1999). In the 1950s and 1960s, special classes in public schools became the preferred educational delivery system for most students with identified disabilities. Contributing to the lack of social and educational change was a common public perception that people with disabilities possessed criminal tendencies because of their genetic makeup (Davies, 1930). Progress was difficult in the face of widespread public prejudice that most people with disabilities had no place in ordinary school and community life. The ongoing discrimination practices, fueled by stereotypes, prejudice, fear of the unfamiliar, paternalization, and pity, continued to disenfranchise people with disabilities in their communities, schools, and workplaces (Brief of Amicus Curiae, Paralyzed Veterans of America, National Organization on Disability, National Mental Health Association, and National Alliance for the Mentally Ill, 2000). Also, residential institutions and special schools remained the norm for educating students with sensory and physical disabilities. Students with severe or profound developmental disabilities generally were still denied educational services of any type; they resided primarily in the back wards of large state institutions.

Civil Rights and Public Education

Charles Houston played a pivotal role in breaking down segregation-ist barriers in higher education. Through Houston's efforts, the University of Maryland law school and the University of Missouri law school were desegregated in 1936 and 1938, respectively. In addition, he encouraged law school graduates to put discriminatory policies and procedures to the constitutional test using the 14th amendment, which led to the conception of the civil rights law (Carter, 2004).

Further progress was made as increased recognition and respect for the dignity of all citizens—regardless of their individual differences—developed in the 1950s and 1960s after the United States had recovered from a severe economic depression and two world wars. There was powerful momentum away from more segregated options for educating minority students. In the landmark court case of the era, the 1954 *Brown v. Board of Education,* Chief Justice Earl Warren ruled that "separate is not equal." That Supreme Court decision invalidated state laws requiring or permitting racial segregation in primary and secondary schools. It was this case that also led toward an increased study of exclusionary policies for students with disabilities in later decades (Stainback, 2002).

The *Brown* case led parents of students with disabilities to organize in groups such as the National Association for Retarded Citizens (now known as The Arc) and to initiate advocacy activities for educating their children. As a result of the persistence of those parents, Congress authorized funds in 1958 to support preparing special education teachers (Kliewer, 1998). A group of special education leaders (see Blatt, 1969; Dunn, 1968; Dybwad, 1964; Goldberg & Cruickshank, 1958; Hobbs, 1966; Lilly, 1970; Reynolds, 1962; Wolfensberger, 1972) also began advocating for the rights of students with disabilities to learn alongside their nondisabled peers in more normalized school environments. The restrictions imposed by segregated settings such as institutions, special schools, and special classes were viewed, for the first time on a fairly widespread basis, as problematic (Taylor & Blatt, 1999).

Education in the Least Restrictive Environment

In the 1970s, the natural sequel to the thinking engendered by *Brown v. Board of Education* (Warren, 1954) for students with disabilities began to be widely enacted in the U.S. legal system. Court decisions in Pennsylvania in 1971 and the District of Columbia in 1972 established the right of all children labeled as "mentally retarded" to a free and appropriate education and made it more difficult for students with disabilities to be excluded from public schools. In 1973, the Rehabilitation Act, Section 504, and later amendments guaranteed the rights of people with disabilities in employment settings and in educational institutions that receive federal monies. Subsequently, because of pressure by parents, courts, and legislatures, Public Law (P.L.) 94–142 (Education for All Handicapped Children Act) was passed in 1975 and enacted in 1978. That law, now the Individuals with Disabilities Education Act (IDEA), stipulates that no child, regardless of disability, can be denied an appropriate public education in the least restrictive environment (LRE). Spurred by the passage of P.L. 94–142, by 1976 all states had passed laws subsidizing public school programs for students with disabilities. The 1990 reauthorization of IDEA (P.L. 101–476) required that placement of students with disabilities be based on identified needs rather than categorical labels (Villa & Thousand, 2000). Subsequently, IDEA amendments of 1997 (P.L. 105–171) addressed the need for high standards of educational performance for *all* students and teachers, including those in special education.

General Education of All Students

By the early 1980s, students considered to have mild or moderate disabilities were usually integrated into general education classrooms on at least a part-time basis. Furthermore, many students who had not been served in the past (i.e., those considered to have severe disabilities) increasingly began to receive educational services in their local neighborhood schools with involvement in general activities such as the cafeteria, playground, library, halls, buses, and restrooms (Certo, Haring, & York, 1984; Knoblock, 1982; Lusthaus, 1988; Stainback & Stainback, 1984; Villa & Thousand, 1988).

In 1986, the U.S. Office of Special Education and Rehabilitation Services in the U.S. Department of Education issued the Regular Education Initiative (Will, 1986). The purpose of the initiative was to find ways for students with mild and moderate disabilities to be educated in general education classrooms by encouraging special education and other specialized programs to partner with general education. Attention quickly turned to educating *all* students, including those with severe disabilities, in the mainstream of general education (Forest, 1987; Sapon-Shevin, Pugach, & Lilly, 1987; Stainback & Stainback, 1990, 1992; Strully, 1986; Villa & Thousand, 1992). Federal law in the form of the Educate America Act of 1994 (P.L. 103–227) emphasized that educational goals must apply to all students, including those traditionally excluded from educational reforms.

By the end of the 1980s, the merger of special and general education into a single comprehensive system was hotly debated by increasing numbers of professional educators and parents (Gartner & Lipsky, 1987; Stainback & Stainback, 1984, 1992; Thousand & Villa, 1991; York & Vandercook, 1988). On one end of the spectrum, advocacy for and experimentation with actually including students who have severe and profound disabilities began in the general education classrooms on part-time and full-time bases (Forest, 1987; Stainback & Stainback, 1988; Strully & Strully, 1985; Thousand & Villa, 1988). On the other end, attempts were made to slow, stop, and even reverse that trend. Despite mandates for placing students in least restrictive environments, some states have shown little progress, even in the face of lawsuits and federal intervention. Some scholars and researchers continue to argue against inclusion (Fox & Ysseldyke, 1997; Fuchs & Fuchs, 1994; Fuchs, Fuchs, Karms, Hamlett, Katzaroff, & Dutka, 1997; Kauffman, 1993, 1995, 1996, 1997, 1999; Kauffman, Gerber, & Semmel, 1988; Lieberman, 1988; MacMillan, Gresham, & Forness, 1996). They maintain that grouping students with disabilities together allows for more efficient instruction, less disruption of the general education classroom, and opportunities for children with disabilities to affiliate with other children with disabilities. James Kauffman (1995), a prominent figure in special education, opposes inclusion on the following grounds:

> In subhuman ecologies, the concept of the "natural" order also applies. . . . [T]he individual is not essential to ecological balance or to what is considered acceptable. There are sacrificial lambs. We do not want to prevent the fox from eating the mouse, nor do we want to prevent the harsh domination of one primate by another in its natural environment. The individual's life is expendable, and the individual's social standing in the group is accepted, whether the individual is a despot or an outcast. . . . Unfortunately, the ideology of full inclusion . . . ignores or distorts the responsibilities we have to construct the most habitatively restrictive environments we can for our students. (pp. 8–9, 14) *Interesting...*

However, as in the past, such arguments have done little to slow the overall recognition and trend toward achieving inclusive education. The movement toward including all students within the full range of diversity in the mainstream of general education has gained unparalleled momentum in recent years. Whereas less than a decade ago we saw only a handful of examples of full inclusion, today numerous examples abound throughout the United States and other countries where students with the most profound cognitive and multiple disabilities have been fully and successfully placed in mainstream elementary and secondary schools. By 1993, every state was implementing inclusion at some level (Webb, 1994). Students ages 6–21 with disabilities increased from 32.8 percent in 1990–91 to 46 percent in 1995–96 (Villa & Thousand, 2000) in general education classrooms.

The inclusive education movement also gained momentum outside special education circles. Articles on how inclusion can be accomplished have been published in widely circulated magazines and newspapers, including *USA Today* and *The Wall Street Journal* ("Full Inclusion," 1993; "More Schools," 1994) and leading general education journals such as *Educational Leadership,* which dedicated the entire October 2003 issue (volume 61, no. 2) to "Teaching All Students." Key educational organizations have conducted studies and proposed resolutions and policy changes supportive of inclusive education. For example, one of six resolutions passed in 1992 by the Association for Supervision and Curriculum Development was for full inclusion of special programs through instructional environments that eliminate tracking and segregation. Such services should focus on prevention of learning problems rather than after-the-fact labeling, on minimal restrictive regulations, and on flexible use of funding to promote success for all children. After studying special education and general education school reform movements for two years, a National Association of School Boards of Education (NASBE, 1992) study group on special education issued a report titled *Winners All: A Call for Inclusive Schools*. The report urged the creation of a unified educational system through major changes in organizational and instructional practices, preservice and inservice personnel preparation, licensure, and funding.

In 1995, eight additional large and influential educational associations—the National Education Association, American Association of School Administrators, Council for Exceptional Children, Council for Great City Schools, National Association of Elementary School Principals, National Association of Secondary School Principals, National Association of State Directors for Special Education, and National State Board Association—joined NASBE to develop a list of characteristics that enable schools to implement inclusive education practices fully and successfully (Council for Exceptional Children, 1995). In 1997, the National Education Association included in its policies and practices statement this assertion: "There is a growing body of evidence that integration can help provide all students with curricular and life skills that expand their opportunities for future success" (National Education Association, 1997, p. 4).

Research also indicates that general education is taking a leading role in embracing inclusion (Smith & Fox, 2003). Examples of strategic general education programs that include principles and procedures inherent in developing inclusive communities within schools are the Accelerated School Program (Keller, 1995; Levin, 1987), Coalition of Essential Schools (O'Neil, 1995), Success for All Program (Slavin, 1997; Slavin & Madden, 2001), Schoolwide Enrichment Model (Renzulli & Reis, 2001), and Project Zero (Gardner & Perkins, 2002).

Courts have also been increasingly called on to render judgments regarding inclusion. In the landmark case of *Oberti v. Clementon* (1993), U.S. Circuit Court Judge Edward R. Becker ordered the inclusion of a student with severe disabilities. He wrote, "We construe IDEA's mainstreaming requirement to prohibit a school from placing a child with disabilities outside of a regular classroom if education of the child in the regular classroom, with supplementary aids and support services, can be achieved satisfactorily." Since that time, numerous court cases have supported students in general education.

In summary, the number of schools attempting to actualize the vision of inclusive education has grown rapidly. Literature also has emerged that describes the operation of effective inclusive schools (Gartner & Lipsky, 2002; Pujolás, 2003; Stone, 2001; Villa, Thousand, Paolucci-Whitcomb, & Nevin, 1990; Villa, Thousand, Stainback, & Stainback, 1992); methods for differentiating curriculum, instruction, and assessment (Bender, 2002; Downing, 2002; Gregory & Chapman, 2001; Gardner & Perkins, 2002; Heacox, 2001; Levine, 2002; Moll, 2003; Tomlinson, 1999, 2001); and methods for reorganizing the traditional schooling paradigm (Charney, 2002; Friend, 2000; Glasser, 1998; Hammeken, 2000; Jacobs, Power, & Inn, 2002; Kagan & Kagan, 2000; Rubin, 2002; Stainback, 2002; Thousand, Villa, & Nevin, 2002; Villa & Thousand, 1992, 2000; Villa, 2002).

The 1990s inclusion debate has become a total school reform dialogue, inclusive practices have spread throughout the country and the world, and inclusive educational policies and procedures have developed to ensure success (Stainback, 2003). Despite the progress, there remain barriers to be overcome. Not the least among them is the No Child Left Behind Act of 2001 (P.L. 107–110) that, as Julian Bond (2004) points out, is but another setback in the quest for equity in education. However, there is growing recognition of concerns such as those engendered in P.L. 107–110, including the debilitating effects of standardization, the "one size fits all" philosophy, and allowing money and supports to be removed from those schools that most need it (e.g. Carroll & Taber, 1999; Kohn & Shannon, 2002; Lent & Tipkin, 2003; Tomlinson, 2002). This growing recognition will provide insight and guidance to help avoid such pitfalls in the future.

● ● ● ● ●

With this progress pending, we now must begin to focus on and move toward the next milepost in our quest for "best educational practices." Moving beyond desegregation, mainstreaming, integration, and inclusion, we can naturally progress toward and embrace the inherent potential values of unity (Stainback, 2004).

As Gandhi once stated, "Our ability to reach unity in diversity will be the beauty and test of our civilization" (Carroll & Taber, 1999, p. 4). Recognizing and capitalizing on the beauty and power of all diversity can be nurtured in our schools. Treating everyone with dignity and respect, valuing cooperation, and promoting mutual support and responsibility toward our fellow community members are just a few of the practices for promoting unity that have been proposed (Carroll & Taber, 1999; Charney, 1997, 2002; Cushman, 1994; Delpit, 1995; Noddings, 1992) and are beginning to gain attention in our schools.

Unity involves building on the diversity inherent in each person to bring strength to the whole, while maintaining respect and support for the individual. In sum, it recognizes our unity, our interconnectedness and our responsibility to both ourselves and others to make things better for everyone. This is a step that has been gradually forming for more than a decade due to the work of caring educators, and it will move education beyond the current inclusion phase into the next phase of the "dream."

In a treatise written during the late 1800s, when violent changes were being precipitated by the Industrial Revolution in England, James Allen (1992, pp. 3–4) pointed out, "The greatest achievement was at first a dream. . . . Dreams are the seedlings of reality. . . . If you but remain true to them, your world will at last be built." As with any dream worthy of pursuit, there have been—and will continue to be—many challenges and barriers. They are not insurmountable reasons to abandon the dream, but are simply problems to be solved.

References

Ainscow, M. (Ed.). (1991). *Effective schools for all.* London: David Fulton Publishers.

Allen, J. (1992). *As a man thinketh.* New York: Barnes and Noble.

Anderson, R. (1998). Attitudes toward educators with disabilities. In R. Anderson, C. Keller, & J. Karp (Eds.), *Enhancing diversity: Educators with disabilities.* Washington, DC: Gallaudet University Press.

Association for Supervision and Curriculum Development. (1992). *Resolutions 1992.* Alexandria, VA: Association for Supervision and Curriculum Development.

Bender, W. (2002) *Differentiating instruction for students with learning disabilities.* Port Chester, NY: National Professional Resources.

Blankenship, C., & Lilly, S. (1981). *Mainstreaming students with learning and behavior problems.* New York: Holt, Rinehart and Winston.

Blatt, B. (1969). *Exodus from pandemonium.* Boston: Allyn and Bacon.

Bond, J. (2004). Keynote address presented at the NAACP 95th Annual Convention, Philadelphia, PA.

Brief of Amicus Curiae, Paralyzed Veterans of America, National Organization on Disability, National Mental Health Association, and National Alliance for the Mentally Ill, in Support of Respondents to the Supreme Court, August 11, 2000.

Carroll, L., & Tober, J. (1999). *The indigo children.* Carlsbad, CA: Hay House Publications.

Carter, R. L. (2004). The long road to equity. *The Nation, 278*(17), 28–30.

Certo, N., Haring, N., & York, R. (Eds.). (1984). *Public school integration of severely handicapped students.* Baltimore: Paul H. Brookes.

Charney, R. S. (1997). *Habits of goodness.* Greenfield, MA: NEFC.

Charney, R. S. (2002). *Teaching children to care.* Greenfield, MA: NEFC.

Chaves, I. M. (1977). Historical overview of special education in the United States. In P. Bates, T. L. West, & R. B. Schmerl (Eds.), *Mainstreaming: Problems, potentials and perspectives* (pp. 25–41). Minneapolis, MN: National Support Systems Project.

Council for Exceptional Children. (1995). *Inclusive schools: Lessons from ten schools.* Reston, VA: Author.

Cushman, K. (1994). Empowering students: Essential school's missing link. *Horace, 11*(1), 5–17.

Davies, S. P. (1930). *Social control of the mentally deficient.* New York: Thomas Y. Crowell.

Delpit, L. (1995). *Other people's children: Cultural conflict in the classroom.* New York: New Press.

Downing, J. (2002). *Including students with severe and multiple disabilities in typical classrooms: Practical strategies for teachers* (2nd ed.). Baltimore: Paul H. Brookes.

Dunn, L. M. (1968). Special education for the mildly retarded—Is much of it justifiable? *Exceptional Children, 35*(1), 5–22.

Dybwad, G. (1964). *Challenges in mental retardation.* New York: Columbia University Press.

Fonder, E., & Kennedy, R. (2004). Brown at 50. *The Nation, 278*(17), 15–17.

Forest, M. (1987). Start with the right attitude. *Entourage, 2*(2), 11–13.

Fox, N., & Ysseldyke, J. (1997). Implementing inclusion at the middle school level: Lessons from a negative example. *Exceptional Children, 64*(1), 81–98.

Friend, M. (2000). *Complexities of collaboration.* Port Chester, NY: National Professional Resources.

Fuchs, D., & Fuchs, L. (1994). Inclusive schools movement and the radicalization of special education reform. *Exceptional Children, 60*(4), 294–309.

Fuchs, L., Fuchs, D., Karms, K., Hamlett, C., Katzaroff, M., & Dutka, S. (1997). Effects of task-focused goals on low-achieving students with and without learning disabilities. *American Educational Research Journal, 34*(2), 513–543.

Full inclusion for the disabled in the public schools. (1993, April 21). *USA Today.*

Gardner, H., & Perkins, D. (2002). *Educating for understanding: Project Zero* [Videotape series]. Port Chester, NY: National Professional Resources.

Gartner, A., & Lipsky, D. (1987). Beyond special education. *Harvard Educational Review, 57*(4), 367–395.

Gartner, A., & Lipsky, D. (2002). *Inclusion: A service not a place. A whole school approach.* Port Chester, NY: National Professional Resources.

Glasser, W. (1998). *Building a quality school.* [Video tape series]. Chatsworth, CA: The Glasser Institute.

Goldberg, I., & Cruickshank, W. M. (1958). The trainable but noneducable: Whose responsibility? *National Education Association Journal, 47*(4), 622.

Gregory, G., & Chapman, C. (2001). *Differential instructional strategies: One size doesn't fit all.* Port Chester, NY: National Professional Resources.

Hammeken, P. (2000). *Inclusion.* Port Chester, NY: National Professional Resources.

Heacox, D. (2001). *Differentiated instruction: How to reach and teach all.* Port Chester, NY: National Professional Resources.

Hobbs, N. (1966). Helping the disturbed child: Psychological and ecological strategies. *American Psychologist, 21*(8), 1105–1115.

Hooks, B. (2000). Where we stand: Class matters. New York: Routledge.

Individuals with Disabilities Education Act (IDEA) Amendments of 1997, P.L. 105–17, 20 U.S.C. §§ 1400 *et seq.*

Individuals with Disabilities Education Act (IDEA) of 1990, P.L. 101–476, 20 U.S.C. §§ 1400 *et seq.*

Jacobs, G., Power, M., & Inn, L. (2002). *The teacher sourcebook for cooperative learning.* Port Chester, NY: National Professional Resources.

Kagan, S., & Kagan, L. (2000). *Reaching standards through cooperative learning* [Videotape series]. Port Chester, NY: National Professional Resources.

Kauffman, J. M. (1993). How we might achieve the radical reform of special education. *Exceptional Children, 60*(3), 294–309.

Kauffman, J. M. (1995, April). *Why we must celebrate a diversity of restrictive environments.* Keynote address presented at the Annual Convention of the Council for Exceptional Children (April), Indianapolis, IN.

Kauffman, J. M. (1996). The challenge of nihilism. *TEASE, 19,* 205–206.

Kauffman, J. M. (1997). Caricature, science, and exceptionality. *Remedial and Special Education, 18*(3), 130–132.

Kauffman, J. M. (1999). How we prevent the prevention of emotional and behavioral disorders. *Exceptional Children, 65*(4), 448–468.

Kauffman, J. M., Gerber, M., & Semmel, M. (1988). Arguable assumptions underlying the regular education initiative. *Journal of Learning Disabilities, 21*(1), 6–11.

Keller, B. (1995). Accelerated schools: Hands-on learning in a unified community. *Educational Leadership, 52*(5), 10–13.

Kliewer, C. (1998). The meaning of inclusion. *Mental Retardation, 36*(4), 317–321.

Knoblock, P. (1982). *Teaching and mainstreaming autistic children.* Denver, CO: Love Publishing.

Kohn, A., & Shannon, P. (2002). *Education, Inc.: Turning learning into a business.* Portsmouth, NH: Heinemann Publications.

Lent, R. C., & Tipkin, G. (2003). *Silent no more: Voices of courage in American schools.* Portsmouth, NH: Heinemann Publications.

Levin, H. (1987). Accelerated schools for disadvantaged students. *Educational Leadership, 44*(6), 19–21.

Levine, M. (2002). *A mind at a time.* Port Chester, NY: National Professional Resources.

Lieberman, L. (1988). *Preserving special education for those who need it.* Newtonville, MA: GloWorm Publications.

Lilly, S. (1970). Special education: A tempest in a teapot. *Exceptional Children, 37*(1), 43–49.

Lusthaus, E. (1988). Education integration . . . letting our children go. *Journal of the Association for the Severely Handicapped, 14*(1), 6–7.

MacMillan, D., Gresham, F., & Forness, S. (1996). Full inclusion: An empirical perspective. *Behavioral Disorders, 21*(2), 145–159.

Moll, A. (2003). *Differentiating instruction guide for inclusive teaching.* Port Chester, NY: National Professional Resources.

More schools embrace full inclusion of the disabled. (1994, April 13). *Wall Street Journal.*

NASBE Study Group on Special Education. (1992, October). *Winners all: A call for inclusive schools.* Alexandria, VA: National Association of State Boards of Education.

National Education Association. (1997). *The integration of students with special needs into regular classrooms: Policies and practices that work.* Washington, DC: Author.

Noddings, N. (1992). *The challenge to care in schools: An alternative approach to education.* New York: Teachers College Press.

Oberti v. Board of Education of Clementon, New Jersey, No. 92-5462 (3rd Cir. May 28, 1993).

O'Neil, J. (1995). On lasting school reform: A conversation with Tom Sizer. *Educational Leadership, 52*(5), 14–19.

Pujolás, P. (2003). *Aprendre junts alumnes diferents: Els eauips d'aprenentatge cooperatiu a l'aula.* Catalonia, Spain: University of Vic.

Racino, J. (1999). *Policy, program evaluation, and research in disability: Community support for all.* New York: Hawthorne Press.

Renzulli, J., & Reis, S. (2001). *The Schoolwide Enrichment Model.* Port Chester, NY: National Professional Resources.

Reynolds, M. C. (1962). Framework for considering some issues in special education. *Exceptional Children, 28*(3), 367–370.

Reynolds, M. C., & Birch, J. W. (1988). *Adaptive mainstreaming.* New York: Longman.

Rubin, H. (2002). *Collaborative leadership.* Thousand Oaks, CA: Sage Publications.

Sapon-Shevin, M., Pugach, M., & Lilly, S. (1987, November). *Moving toward merger: Implications for general and special education.* Paper presented at the 10th Annual CEC Teacher Education Division Conference, Arlington, VA.

Scherer, M. (Ed.). (2003, October). Teaching all students. *Educational Leadership, 61* (2).

Sigmon, S. (1983). The history and future of educational segregation. *Journal for Special Educators, 19*(4), 1–13.

Slavin, R. (1997). Including inclusion in school reform: Success for All and Roots and Wings. In D. Lipsky & A. Gartner (Eds.), *Inclusion and school reform: Transforming America's classrooms* (pp. 375–387). Baltimore: Paul H. Brookes.

Slavin, R., & Madden, N. (2001). *One million children: Success for All.* Port Chester, NY: National Professional Resources.

Smith, J. K., & Fox, M. J. (2003, January). *Decolonizing our way to inclusion.* Paper presented at the conference of the Comparative and International Education Society, Honolulu, HI.

Stainback, S. (2002). The inclusion movement: A goal for restructuring education. In M. Winzer & K. Mazurek (Eds.), *Special education in the 21st century: Issues of inclusion and reform.* Washington, DC: Gallaudet University Press.

Stainback, S. (2003). Prologue. In P. Pujolás (Ed.), *Aprendre junts alumnes diferents: Els eauips d'aprenentatge cooperatiu a l'aula.* Catalonia, Spain: University of Vic.

Stainback, S. (2004). *Equity to unity.* W. L. Bradsher Distinguished Chair Presentation. Winston Salem State University, Winston Salem, NC.

Stainback, S., & Stainback, W. (1988). Educating students with severe disabilities in regular classes. *Teaching Exceptional Children, 21*(1), 16–19.

Stainback, S., & Stainback, W. (1990). *Support networks for inclusive schooling.* Baltimore: Paul H. Brookes.

Stainback, S., & Stainback, W. (1992). *Curriculum considerations for inclusive classrooms.* Baltimore: Paul H. Brookes.

Stainback, W., & Stainback, S. (1984). A rationale for the merger of special and regular education. *Exceptional Children, 51*(2), 102–111.

Stainback, W., & Stainback, S. (1992). *Controversial issues confronting special education.* Boston: Allyn and Bacon.

Stone, R. (2001). *Best practices for high school classrooms.* Thousand Oaks, CA: Sage Publications.

Strully, J. (1986). *Our children and the regular education classroom, or why settle for anything less than the best?* Paper presented at the 1986 annual conference of the Association for Persons with Severe Handicaps, San Francisco.

Strully, J., & Strully, C. (1985). Teach your children. *Canadian Journal on Mental Retardation, 35*(4), 3–11.

Taylor, S., & Blatt, S. (Eds.). (1999). *In search of the promised land: The collected papers of Burton Blatt.* Washington, DC: American Association on Mental Retardation.

Thousand, J. S., & Villa, R. A. (1988). Enhancing educational success through collaboration, *IMPACT, 1*(2), 14.

Thousand, J. S., & Villa, R. A. (1991). A futuristic view of the REI: A response to Jenkins, Pious, and Jewell. *Exceptional Children, 57*, 556–562.

Thousand, J. S., Villa, R. A., & Nevin, A. I. (Eds.). (2002). *Creativity and collaborative learning: The practical guide to empowering students, teachers, and families* (2nd ed.). Baltimore: Paul H. Brookes.

Tomlinson, C. A. (1999). *The differentiated classroom.* Alexandria, VA: ASCD.

Tomlinson, C. A. (2001). *How to differentiate instruction in mixed-ability classrooms.* Port Chester, NY: National Professional Resources.

Tomlinson, C. A. (2002). Proficiency is not enough. *Education Week, 22*(10), 36, 38.

Villa, R. A. (2002). *Collaboration for inclusion* [Videotape series]. Port Chester, NY: National Professional Resources.

Villa, R. A., & Thousand, J. S. (1988). Enhancing success in heterogeneous classrooms and schools: The powers of partnership. *Teacher Education and Special Education, 11*(4), 144–154.

Villa, R. A., & Thousand, J. S. (1992). How one district integrated special and regular education. *Educational Leadership, 50*(2), 39–41.

Villa, R. A., & Thousand, J. S. (Eds.) (2000). *Restructuring for a caring and effective education: Piecing the puzzle together.* (2nd ed.). Baltimore: Paul H. Brookes.

Villa, R., Thousand, J., Paolucci-Whitcomb, M., & Nevin, A. (1990). In search of a new paradigm for collaborative consultation. *Journal of Educational and Psychological Consultation, 1*(4), 279–292.

Villa, R. A., Thousand, J. S., Stainback, W., & Stainback, S. (Eds) (1992*). Restructuring for caring and effective education: An administrative guide to creating heterogeneous schools.* Baltimore: Paul H. Brookes.

Warren, E. (1954). Brown v. Board of Education of Topeka, 347 U.S. 483, 493.

Webb, N. (1994). Special education: With new court decisions behind them, advocates see inclusion as a question of values. *Harvard Educational Letter, 10*(4), 1–3.

Will, M. (1986). Educating students with learning problems—A shared responsibility. *Exceptional Children, 52*(5), 411–416.

Wolfensberger, W. (1972). *The principle of normalization in human services.* Toronto, Canada: National Institute on Mental Retardation.

York, J., & Vandercook, T. (Eds.). (1988). Integrated education. *IMPACT, 1*(2).

From My Friend, Ro Vargo

Rosalind Vargo and Joe Vargo

A school should not be a preparation for life. A school should be life.

—Elbert Hubbard

It was Tuesday, a beautiful autumn morning at Syracuse University. Ro had just finished her class "Topics in American Music—20th Century" in Bowne Hall and was walking back to the car (with my assistance) to go home. Joe, Ro's dad, was waiting in the car. He and I looked at each other and at Ro and wondered how we had gotten here. After all, it seemed like only yesterday. . . .

Kindergarten

Among our vivid memories is kindergarten and Ro's first invitation to a birthday party. Kristen's mother phoned to ask if she should make any special arrangements for Ro to attend. Fighting back tears, we responded, "No, but thanks for asking." Kristen's mom said her daughter was so looking forward to Ro coming. Then we said it: "We love Ro because she's our daughter. But do you know why other kids like her?"

The mom replied, "Well, I can speak only for my daughter, Kristen. She says she likes Ro's smile and that Ro is someone you can really talk to . . . and that she wears really neat clothes." Kristen's mom continued, "I think kids like Ro because she isn't a threat to them; they can just be themselves around her."

2nd Grade

In 2nd grade, we invited several kids to Ro's birthday party. Because we would be picking them up at school, we needed to know who would be coming. The night before the party, we called Eric's mom and politely asked, "Is Eric coming to Ro's party tomorrow?"

She said, "I'm sorry I didn't call you, but Eric said he just told Ro in school yesterday that he was coming. Was that all right?" It was more than all right! To Eric, the fact that Ro couldn't talk didn't mean that she couldn't understand him.

Shortly thereafter, while attending Mass on Sunday, we reflected on how feverishly we had worked to get Ro into regular school to expose her to real-life learning and living. We began to feel guilty about why we had not persevered in getting Ro involved in our church as well. Because Ro was regularly going to Mass now, we thought it might be the right time to approach our pastor about having Ro receive First Holy Communion with her age-mates.

Somewhat apprehensive, we met one evening with the pastor, bringing Ro along. Thinking we would have to justify her inclusion, we had our appropriate scriptural references and detailed notes to build our case. To our surprise and delight, our pastor agreed wholeheartedly. He said, "You know, we are the ones with the hang-ups, not Ro. We make all the rules so that people like Ro can't receive Communion." He continued, "You know, I'm excited about Ro receiving our Lord, but I am even more excited about what effect Ro will have on our lives and our parish families' lives when she does."

When First Communion Day came and Ro approached the altar, her dad, Joe, recalls being unable to talk or move after she received Communion. His feelings were testimony to what had happened not just for Ro but for many of us. The liturgy ended with hugs, kisses, and tears of renewed belief that Christ was alive in our midst through Ro. A non-Catholic friend, unaware of the spiritual significance of the day for us, said she was intensely moved by seeing Ro in a seemingly transfixed state. Her reaction brought back memories of our pastor's words about the potential effect of Ro's Communion on others' lives.

4th Grade

In 4th grade, a time when pressure to have the "right" clothes and hairstyles had already begun, Ro was voted "Best Friend" by her 25 "typical" 4th-grade classmates. Somehow, Ro's inclusion in the school life was making a tremendous difference in many kids as well. Her "giftedness" was recognized and celebrated.

We recall another night when a puzzling phone call came for Ro. Sharing the same nickname as my daughter, I thought the call was for me and I replied, "Speaking."

The young girl at the other end of the line clarified, "No, I'd like the Ro who goes to Ed Smith School."

I said, "Hold on," and exclaimed to Joe, "Someone wants to talk with Ro on the phone!" We got Ro from the dinner table and put the phone to her ear. Immediately recognizing the voice of her friend Ghadeer, Ro started laughing. She then nodded her head to indicate "yes" and followed with a head shake indicating "no." Curiosity got the best of me and I took the phone, reporting to Ghadeer, "Ro's listening and nodding her head."

Ghadeer said, "Great, I'm asking her advice about a birthday present for a friend. Now, did she nod 'yes' for the jewelry or 'yes' for the board game?"

Ro's 11th Birthday

We remember with pleasure Ro's 11th birthday party. Before the party, the mother of one of Ro's friends called to ask if the present she had picked out for Ro was OK. Apparently, her daughter hadn't been with her when she went shopping. She had just wrapped it and given it to her daughter to take to school that morning. She wasn't sure if the gift was the "in" thing and feared that her daughter would die of embarrassment if it weren't.

She had bought a jump rope for Ro—a deluxe model. Without hesitation, I said that it was a wonderful idea and a gift that Ro would love using with her sisters.

29

With a sigh of relief, the mom responded, "Well, I am glad. I was hoping that Ro was not handicapped or anything. Is she?"

For the life of me, I wanted to say "No" and save this mom obvious embarrassment. So I said, "Well, a little bit." After many of her apologies and my reassurances, we got off the phone as friends. She had made my day, my week, my life! The thought that an 11-year-old girl had received a birthday party invitation, wanted to go, and asked her mom to buy a present, *never thinking it important to mention that her friend had a disability,* still makes me cry with wonder and happiness.

A later message of acceptance and love came at the birthday party itself when Ro opened the present. Remember that the girl had no idea what her mom had bought. She did know that her friend Ro had three occupational therapy and three physical therapy sessions a week and attended an adaptive physical education class.

When Ro unwrapped the jump rope, all the girls were elated, shrieking, "I hope I get one of those for my birthday," and "Oh, cool." The girls immediately dragged Ro down the stairs and outside to the driveway, where they tied one end of the jump rope to her wrist. With the strength of her twirling partner, Ro was able to rotate the rope for her friends. It was Ro's best adaptive occupational therapy activity in months.

A Gift for Ghadeer

Probably the most profound testimony to inclusive education occurred in January 1993. Ghadeer, Ro's friend who had called to ask for advice on gift selection, suffered a cerebral hemorrhage, or severe stroke. At the age of 12, she was comatose for almost four weeks. Teachers had prepared classmates, including Ro, for Ghadeer's imminent death. However, after weeks of having family, teachers, and friends read at her bedside, Ghadeer miraculously, although not completely, recovered. Her voice and articulation were so severely impaired that she could not communicate orally. To the amazement of the child's doctors and nurses, her disability did not stop her from communicating; she began to use sign language. An interpreter was quickly found who asked Ghadeer, "Where did you learn sign language?"

Ghadeer replied in sign, "From my friend, Ro Vargo!"

After four months of intensive rehabilitative therapy, Ghadeer returned to school, but now as a "special education" student requiring speech and language services plus physical and occupational therapy. Her family proudly reports that Ghadeer turned away the "special" bus and rode the regular school bus on her first day back to school. Furthermore, she advocated for herself to get a laptop computer to assist her with her schoolwork. Inclusive education enabled Ghadeer to get to know someone like Ro and to learn about augmentative communication systems and her rights, particularly her right to be part of her school, class, and friendship circle. She had learned that a person can still belong even if something unexpected—like a disability—happens.

What's Hard About Being Ro's Friend?

Ghadeer was one of many of Ro's friends who became quite capable of articulating for themselves what Ro meant to them and the kinds of things that they learned at school with her. That relationship became clear when Ro and a group of her friends responded to questions from parents and teachers in a session titled "Building Friendships in an Inclusive Classroom" at a national education conference that they attended.

Tiffany said, "I think Ro should be in class with all of us because how else is Ro going to learn the really important stuff? Besides, we can learn a lot from her."

Teachers asked Ro's friends some unusual questions, such as, "'Have you ever discussed her disability with her?'"

Stacey replied, "No, I know she is different, but I never thought it important to ask. Like, for instance, I never thought to go up to a black kid in my class and say, 'You're black. How come you're different?'"

A "popular" question among teachers and parents—judging by their nods—was "What is the hardest thing about being Ro's friend?" As Ro's parents, we held our breath, waiting for responses such as "She drools," "She walks funny," or "She's a messy eater."

But again Stacey spoke up, saying, "The hardest thing about being Ro's friend is that she always has a parent or an adult with her." Ouch! That hurt. But Stacey's observation taught us, Ro's parents, an important lesson that will surely have a positive effect on our daughter's future.

Transition to Middle School

The transition from elementary to middle school was tough socially for Ro, as it can be for any adolescent. For Ro, the first months were spent in isolation, but her isolation was not one of physical proximity. Ro attended a regular 6th grade program and had to gain acceptance from her new middle school peers. Initially, she was ignored or stared at; a few classmates even teased her. When Ro was assigned to a work group, no group members complained out loud, but Ro noticed nonverbal signs of rejection. In those first months, we began to doubt our decision to include Ro in middle school. We recalled the comment a teacher from the previous year had made: "Middle school kids don't like themselves. How can you expect them to like your kid?"

Mauricha, a classmate, became Ro's closest new friend. It was Mauricha who broke the social barrier. Asked how the two became friends, Mauricha said, "I saw her. She saw me. We've just been friends ever since." One night when I was taking Mauricha home, she looked at me and touched my arm. "You know, Mrs. Vargo," Mauricha said, "lots of teachers think I'm friends with Ro cuz it gets me more attention. That isn't true. The truth is, I need her more than she needs me."

Ro's father and I would have to summarize Ro's middle school experience as fairly typical. When reflecting on our other daughters' experiences in middle school, we realize that there were many of the same issues: isolation at times, hot and cold friendships, recognition of and a growing interest in boys, physical changes, teasing, challenging class work, and parents who didn't know anything! Oh, yes. Ro went to her first dance and danced with Jermaine.

There were three particularly memorable highlights during Ro's last year of middle school: Kristen, Mr. S., and the idea of going off to high school.

Kristen

Kristen joined Ro as her teaching assistant. The two immediately bonded. Kristen connected with Ro in a way that no adult had and understood the vision that we had for Ro. Kristen intuitively knew how to play the support role without getting in Ro's way and her desire to connect with others. Kristen was talented—a gift.

Mr. S.

Mr. S. was the gym teacher. He had the distinction of being the longest-tenured teacher in the building—35 years! He ran a tough gym class and did not tolerate poor behavior or interruptions of any kind. Of course, Ro was assigned to Mr. S.'s class. She qualified immediately as an "interruption." Although Mr. S. was initially against having Ro in his class, he finally agreed—as long as she stayed in the corner with Kristen. As Ro practiced her physical education from afar, she caught the attention of a few students who believed that Ro was having much more fun than they were. Several times, students opted to join Ro during free time, and the numbers grew.

Under the circumstances (and with the help of Joe's and my advocacy), Mr. S. realized that he was going to have to give in and let Ro join the group for fear of losing them all! Over time, Ro won over Mr. S., and he welcomed her to his class. On the last day of school, Ro came home with a whistle around her neck and a note from the principal that read, "Mr. S. retired today after 35 years. He wanted Ro to have his whistle!"

Plans for High School

The staff at the middle school had agreed to work with the staff at Henninger High School to prepare them for the six students with disabilities who would be transitioning to their building in less than a year. The dream of high school captured the imagination of middle school students, and Ro was no exception. One thing that Joe and I learned about this transition was to start the planning process early. We already felt as if we were behind because, although the new teachers had heard of inclusion, they were unfamiliar with the way Ro lived it! Joe and I thought: another school . . . starting over again . . . high school.

Arrival at High School

On September 4, 1996, Ro and six other students with disabilities entered Henninger High School. Early on, Ro communicated, "I like the subject (zoology), and the kids and I have learned a lot. I have had some classes I didn't like. It is hard for me when classes have no small groups and no homework for me. Sometimes there is too much information. The worst is when neither the kids nor the teachers talk to me." Ro traveled to New York City for a weekend with her zoology classmates and teachers to research the zoos and wildlife preserves there.

Inclusive education in high school was offering Ro a whole new world of opportunities and choices. She joined the Key Club, a service organization that met twice a month. She accrued service hours through her volunteer job at a local day-care center. In the fully inclusive day care, Ro was acting as a role model for many young students with disabilities, as well as for the whole class and her fellow workers.

During her early high school years, Ro communicated many things to us in various ways. It was a time of painful sharing, as well as a time for action and reflection. Her "voice" gave us a clearer vision of where and what Ro wanted to do with her life. For example, when Ro developed frequent outbursts, both at home and at school, Joe and I worked with teachers and the school psychologist to get a better handle on what might be going on. One night, Ro's speech therapist phoned us. She had promised Ro that she would call that night and discuss the day's session. Apparently that afternoon, Ro had become quite upset. She had typed something like "I want to go sitter," the letters had spelled out C-i-n-d-e-r-e-l-l-a and something about Aunt Marge, and then she burst out crying. I honestly could not figure out where Ro wanted to go. The pieces were fragmented and made no sense. After I got off the phone, I shared the information with Joe.

He immediately said, "Don't you know what she is talking about?"

I said no.

Joe explained, "She's talking about when Josie, her sister [close to the spelling of 'sitter'], went to the Christmas formal last weekend with Todd."

I didn't know if we should laugh or cry. When Ro woke up the next morning, I asked her if she was upset because she wanted to go to a formal dance with a boy, have Aunt Marge take pictures, and look like Cinderella. She nodded, "Yes." This painful revelation was especially hard for Josie. Early that morning, around toast and coffee, we committed to Ro that she would go to her junior prom, even if it was the last thing we did! From the smile on Ro's face, I think she knew we meant it. (Ro attended not only the junior prom but also the senior ball.)

On the afternoon of her first volunteer job, Ro had to fill out an application. Her teaching assistant completed it with Ro's input. However, 10 minutes later, Ro totally dissolved into a full-blown temper tantrum.

The panicked teaching assistant questioned Ro, "Does it have anything to do with the application?"

Ro nodded, "Yes."

"Was it #1, #2, #3 . . . ." until the question, "What has been your biggest challenge?"

Without consulting Ro, the teaching assistant had written "Rett syndrome." That was the one! Ro wanted it removed. Yes, the line about Rett syndrome.

Another time that Ro clearly expressed her thoughts was when she was nominated by her teachers for Student of the Month. She had to complete an information sheet for the committee who would select the winner. After much deliberation, Ro opted not to include any of her work with local university students and their numerous papers on her life experiences or any of her work with other girls with Rett syndrome. Basically, her nomination went in with just her name, age, and favorite teacher. Ro was making it clear that she didn't think that Rett syndrome was something important to share about herself. It wasn't really who she was, or what she did, or even what she wanted to have.

For her assignment in Health Career class, Ro had to design a poster depicting the occupations that she was interested in pursuing. We had never asked her that question. The family cut out pictures and words for 15 minutes each night for a week, and one member would ask, "Do you want this on your poster?"

Ro would respond, "Yes" or "No." At the end of the week, the final product was amazing. It was full of the faces of people. Ro wanted to work with people. There were no inanimate objects or sports memorabilia. It was as if Ro knew her limitations, but she also knew her strengths. Inclusive education classes were challenging Ro in every way and giving rise to a louder and louder voice.

The voice of Ro's peers was also becoming clearer and louder. While on the zoology trip to New York City, Ro and her dad struggled for three days to keep up with the fast pace of a very busy itinerary. Ro's classmates seemed oblivious to her tiring easily and to the loco-motion problems that caused her to lag behind. It appeared that they hardly noticed her at all that weekend—at least that was Joe's obser-vation. Ro still enjoyed the trip, and it was a wonderful bonding expe-rience for her and dad.

Months later, we came to understand the ramifications and the benefits of Ro's participation in that trip. Students in the class began to vocalize, without our knowledge, concerns about Ro's support person in school. They complained to their teacher at first about how they thought the teaching assistant was disre-spectful to Ro. When the teacher heard their complaints, she noti-fied the principal. When there was no action, kids went to their parents and parents came to us. When the school administration failed to act, Ro's peers did!

The vision for inclusive education was a reality. We had hoped that the kids who sat in class with Ro would not seek to harm her now or in the days to come. We had hoped that they would protect her and take care of her, seek the social and legislative reforms to support the inclusive lifestyle that she had grown accustomed to, and gladly be her neighbors and her friends because they had shared the same space, the same hopes, and the same dreams. Ro and her peers in an inclusive high school setting were already living out the dream, and there was no going back for any of us.

After Ro's third year in high school, the frustration and outbursts returned. Ro was clearly envious of the planning and choices that her sister Josie was engaging in. College visits, college applications, and senior pictures were taking place. We were unclear about what Ro's choices could be, and she communicated that the situation was not fair.

One night I read about an inclusive college setting in Kentucky. Perfect? Students naturally seek postsecondary opportunities. Why not Ro? The ONCAMPUS program had been initiated as a collaborative effort between the Inclusive Elementary and Special Education Program of Syracuse University (SU) and the Syracuse City School District. It was developed to enhance SU's teacher preparation program and the school district's inclusive schooling options. ONCAMPUS brought six high school students ages 19–21 with moderate to severe disabilities to the SU campus where they would participate with other SU students in academic, social, vocational, recreational, and service learning experiences.

Ro's behavior improved immensely. She actively communicated her absolute delight with her peers that she was going to attend SU next year. She decided which courses to take, what clubs to belong to, and where she would eat lunch.

However, getting a handicapped parking permit proved to be no easy task. After much discussion and hassle, Ro was secured her permit. When I picked it up, the receptionist asked, "Oh, is this for Ro Vargo who went to Henninger High School?"

"Yes," I replied.

"Tell her I said 'Hi.'"

"You know Ro?" I asked.

"Yeah, I graduated with her from Henninger last year."

Inclusive education . . . another voice heard and in all the right places . . . another confirmation.

Syracuse University Students

Jacqueline was a sophomore at SU in the School of Social Work. She began to spend time with Ro on campus through her job as a residential habilitation counselor. She shared with Ro the names of all the good professors and the courses she should pass up! Jackie was the voice of experience. As a sophomore in the visual and performing arts program, Jackie was a member of SU's jazz and pep band, as well as the dance band. She would clue Ro in on any musical performances on campus.

Before traveling abroad to study, Ashley spent every Tuesday with Ro for six months, just eating or hanging out. Katie was an SU cheerleader who picked up Ro and took her to class when her day-habilitation person went on vacation. Colleen celebrated Ro's 21st birthday with her on a bar-hopping adventure in a 16-passenger limo!

Justine had seen Ro on campus and had thought to herself, "Boy, Ro looks and acts a lot like my brother who has autism." She was a senior in the Maxwell School of Communication at the time. As part of her final grade, Justine had to produce a short documentary. She approached Ro and asked if she would be willing to be part of a presentation highlighting the ONCAMPUS program. Ro agreed. A relationship developed that spanned a whole year. Justine introduced Ro to Gregg, another senior, who would be the codirector. They met frequently to talk and shoot videotape.

The final project culminated in a video titled *Ro*. Justine and Gregg's perspective was clearly evident in their work. It was respectful, serious, and funny, and Ro's hopes and dreams of being on a university campus were unfolded in the video. The images were searing and thought-provoking as Ro traversed the campus. Justine and Gregg's voice on this tape will last forever, and so will Ro's voice.

Ro's inclusion in high school and college settings has certainly caused my daughter some pain as she acknowledged her limitations and struggled to belong. Yet inclusion also prompted Ro's self-actualization, self-determination, and self-acceptance and her growing belief that there is nothing that she cannot do. Placing herself in a "regular" environment was a risk that Ro was willing to take.

Inclusive education has always been an emotional and physical risk for all of us, especially Ro. But it has clearly been worth it! Now, when the little yellow school bus drives past our house, I strain to hear the voices of inclusion. Today, Ro uses adult services, and we're starting all over again: justifying, rationalizing, sharing vision, relaying data and information.

When parents of children with disabilities become lonely and fatigued, their voices can become silent. There are limited routes of appeal and no federal mandates to support Ro's inclusive lifestyle. Frankly, we are exhausted and frustrated. Nothing prepared us for this new fight to belong in a community outside of school. This adult, segregated mentality has taken its toll. We have been diligent advocates, articulate spokespersons. We've awakened—not only in Ro but also in many other students—the idea that inclusive education can mean college.

The impact of Ro's inclusive education is made clear by the relationships she forged along the way. Ghadeer called Ro to attend Ghadeer's high school graduation party. Remember, Ghadeer was Ro's elementary school friend who told doctors that she had learned sign language from "my friend, Ro Vargo." Well, six years later, she remembered and invited Ro to her party. Ro received a Christmas card from Mauricha, the middle school friend who broke the social barrier for Ro. The note began, "Hi, Ro. I know you probably don't remember me, but I have never forgotten you." Mauricha explained that she was working as a home health aide and taking a sign language course at night.

Kristen, Ro's teaching assistant, married Gavin. Ro was invited to the wedding, and she reminisced with the bridal party about the last time that they had all been in a limo together! It was the night of the senior prom at Henninger, some three years before. Ro carries take-out food to Kristen and Gavin's house once in a while so Kristen doesn't have to cook. In a newspaper article highlighting the June 2002 high school graduations in the area, Kristen told a reporter that she and Ro were very close and that "Ro was the sister I never had." Kristen and Ro tell each other everything, including Kristen's secret that she was going to have a baby.

The Future?

Our "severely impaired" child has already accomplished more than we had ever thought possible, and she continues to grow. Also "growing" are Brandiss, Holly, Jackie, Justine, Katie, Maureen, Mauricha, Nicole, Patty, Quantia, Tyrell, and many others. We believe in those young adults who sat in class with Ro. They will not seek to harm her but will be her community—the ones who will protect and care for her. They will advocate social and legislative reform to support the inclusive lifestyle to which Ro and they have grown accustomed. They will gladly be her neighbors, caretakers, job coaches, and friends because they shared the same classes, space, hopes, and dreams.

Chapter 3

The Rationales for Creating and Maintaining Inclusive Schools

Richard A. Villa and Jacqueline S. Thousand

The Goal of Public Education

There are multiple rationales for advocating inclusive schools. We'd like to explore those rationales by inviting the reader to think about and answer this question: "What do you believe should be the goals of public education? In other words, what are the outcomes, attitudes, dispositions, and skills you want the children you care about to possess by the time they exit high school?" After you have answered that question from your personal or professional perspective, try answering it again—but this time from the perspective of others. Think of students both with identified disabilities and without identified disabilities. Think of adults with roles or concerns in education that differ from your own (e.g., a parent, an educator, an administrator, a school board member, a local businessperson, a community member). What do you notice? Are there commonalities in your responses?

The authors of this chapter have posed that question to tens of thousands of parents, teachers, administrators, students, university professors, and concerned citizens across the Americas, Europe, Asia, and the Middle East. What we have noted is that—regardless of the divergent perspectives, vested interests, or locales of the people queried—their responses are very similar and tend to fall into one or more of the four categories that are shown in Figure 3.1 and are borrowed from Native American culture.

Figure 3.1

Frequently Identified Goals of Public Education, by Category

BELONGING

- Having friends
- Forming and maintaining relationships
- Getting along with others, including coworkers
- Being part of a community
- Being a caring parent and family member

MASTERY

- Having success and becoming competent in something or some things
- Being well rounded
- Being a good problem solver
- Being flexible
- Having motivation
- Being literate
- Using technology
- Being a lifelong learner
- Reaching potential in areas of interest

INDEPENDENCE

- Having choices in work, recreation, leisure, or continued learning
- Possessing confidence to take risks
- Being as independent as possible
- Assuming personal responsibility
- Holding oneself accountable for actions and decisions
- Being able to self-advocate

GENEROSITY

- Being a contributing member of society
- Valuing diversity
- Being empathetic
- Offering compassion, caring, and support to others
- Being a responsible citizen
- Exercising global stewardship

Traditional Native American education was based on the culture's main purpose: to educate and empower its children. The educational philosophy and approach was holistic, with the central goal being to foster a child's *Circle of Courage* (Van Bockern, Brendtro, & Brokenleg, 2000). The circle comprises four educational objectives or components of self-esteem: belonging, mastery, independence, and generosity. As already noted, these four dimensions of education correspond to the responses articulated by concerned citizens worldwide.

Despite the diversity among the people whom we have sampled, they seem to share common beliefs about the desired outcomes for students. Furthermore, those outcomes are the same for children with and without identified challenges. The outcomes listed in Figure 3.1 clearly show that people are telling us that the curriculum must go beyond traditional academic domains to address the concerns so poignantly expressed in Ginott's letter to teachers (see Figure 3.2).

Historically, special education practices have unintentionally interfered with students' opportunity to experience components of the Circle of Courage. For instance, in an effort to foster students' skill development and independence, we have sent them to "specialized" instruction in separate environments. Although it is important for students to develop skills, it is difficult for students to get the message that they belong when they are sent down the hall or to a different school to develop those skills. Almost every theory of motivation (e.g., Glasser, 1986; Maslow, 1970; Van Bockern, Brendtro, & Brokenleg, 2000) stresses the fulfillment of a child's need to belong as critical, if not prerequisite, to a child's motivation to learn. Exclusion or removal of a child from general education, however, instructs the child that belonging is not forthcoming—but is something that must be earned. Removal signals to a child that "I am not good enough to belong as I am. But if I acquire some unknown number of skills, maybe I will be granted the privilege of belonging." Norman Kunc (2000) describes the dilemma:

> The tragic irony . . . is that as soon as we take away students' sense of belonging, we completely undermine their capacity to learn the skills that will enable them to belong. Herein lies the most painful "Catch-22" situation that confronts students with

Figure 3.2

Letter to Teachers

Dear Teacher:

I am a survivor of a concentration camp. My eyes saw what no man should witness.

- Gas chambers built by learned engineers
- Children poisoned by educated physicians
- Infants killed by trained nurses
- Women and babies shot and burned by high school and college graduates

So I am suspicious of education.

My request is this: Help your students become human.

Your efforts must never produce learned monsters, skilled psychopaths, or educated Adolf Eichmanns.

Reading, writing, and arithmetic are important only if they serve to make our children more humane.

Source: Adapted from *Teacher and Child,* by H. Ginott, 1972, New York: Macmillan. Reprinted with permission.

>   disabilities—they can't belong until they learn, but they can't
>   learn because they are prevented from belonging. (p. 88)

For some people, the rationale for changing the organization of schooling comes out of an explicit examination of the goals of public education and the realization that the goals go beyond academics and are the same for all children. That realization, combined with the dilemma of belonging, leads those people to question why we would choose to continue a divided educational system when the consequences of separation are potentially so dire for some children.

This is hard to argue!

Change in Assumptions

How fundamentally different is the organizational structure of many schools today from that of the schools we attended? People to whom we have posed this question often answer, "Not all that much." In contrast, how different is the world our children are entering from the one we entered after high school graduation? Few would deny that it is dramatically different from the pre-Internet, pre–electronic mail, and pre–video game days of the mid–20th century. We are in the midst of an information explosion. The rate of new technological discoveries, cooperative international business, and societal trends—combined with the exponential growth and change in what is "accurate" knowledge—has led to a situation where no one can keep abreast of all there is to know. The 21st century contrasts with 19th- and 20th-century life, in which the school's role was to prepare most children for farm and factory work, to sort out the elite for continuing education, and to induct and homogenize arriving immigrants into an English-speaking and predominantly Anglo-Saxon, Protestant culture.

Assumptions that drove the curricular, instructional, assessment, and organizational practices of schooling in past centuries have changed, thanks to the complexity of 21st-century adult life. Today's schooling must be based on new assumptions about our global, multicultural, and multilingual society and on the skills, attitudes, and dispositions for success in such a society. What skills must our children acquire to adapt to those changes? Educators and employers alike identify as valuable traits such as communication, creative problem solving, interpersonal skills, and an ability to cope with adversity and uncertainty, as well as appreciate and collaborate with the diverse people of the global community. The heart of the 21st-century curriculum is learning *how* to learn, or how to be a lifelong inquirer.

Delivery of the new curriculum requires trying new ways of teaching (e.g., cooperative group learning, differentiation of instruction, active student-directed learning, detracking, focusing on social skills and communication competence, and community service). Those new approaches better meet student needs. When student diversity rather than homogeneity is the reigning assumption, it is possible to accelerate the transformation of schooling practices and to better prepare every student for the future, a future that is *now*.

Efficacy Data

Question: What is the number-one way in which we assess student performance in the United States?
Proposed Answer: Norm-referenced standardized achievement tests.
Question: If we agree with the many thousands of people who have identified belonging, mastery, independence, generosity, communication, and inquiry skills as important goals of education, what are the standardized achievement tests that we use to measure our children's performance in those goal areas?
Proposed Answer: There aren't any.

These questions and proposed answers are intended to highlight that, in education, we do not always measure what we say we value or consider critical for our children's success. What, then, *have* we measured for students receiving special education? What are the results of those measures? As early as the 1980s, research reviews and meta-analyses—known as the special education "efficacy studies" (Lipsky & Gartner, 1989, p. 19)—measured global school performance of students who received special education. The studies showed that separate special education services had little to no positive effects for students regardless of the intensity or type of their disabilities. In a 1994 review of three meta-analyses of effective special education settings, Baker, Wang, and Walberg concluded that "special-needs students educated in regular classes do better academically and socially than comparable students in non-inclusive settings" (p. 34). Their findings held true regardless of disability or grade level. Likewise, Freeman and Alkin (2000), in a review of 36 studies of children with mental retardation, came to the same conclusion. In the employment arena, results reported by the U.S. Department of Education indicated that "across a number of analyses of post-school results, the message was the same: those who spent more time in regular education experienced better results after high school" (1995, p. 87). Researchers have also found that the inclusion of students with severe disabilities did *not* have adverse effects on classmates' academic or behavioral success as measured by standardized tests and report card grades (Hollowood, Salisbury, Rainforth, & Palombaro, 1994; Sharpe, York, & Knight, 1994). Inclusion of students with severe disabilities enhanced their classmates' as well as their own achievement, self-esteem, and school attendance (see Cole & Meyer, 1991; Costello, 1991; Kelly, 1992; Strain, 1983; Straub & Peck, 1994).

It is also well established that students of color are grossly overrepresented in special education; thus, continuing separate education programs has a racist aspect. Scherer (1992/93), for example, reported that African American children are three times more likely to be placed in special education classes than European American children but only half as likely to be placed in advanced or gifted programs.

Overall, the data speak volumes. Federal legislation acknowledges in the Individuals with Disabilities Education Act (IDEA) that

> over 20 years of research and experience [have] demonstrated that the education of children with disabilities can be made more effective by having high expectations and ensuring students' access in the general education curriculum to the maximum extent possible . . . [and] providing appropriate special education and related services and aids and supports in the regular classroom to such children, whenever possible. (20 U.S.C. § 1400(c)(5))

Legal Issues

In response to increased advocacy for including children with disabilities in general education, many people ask whether the law has recently changed. The answer is, "No." Since IDEA was initially promulgated in 1975, the law and subsequent reauthorizations have reflected Congress's preference for educating children with disabilities in general education classrooms with their peers. What has changed is the know-how of teachers, administrators, and communities. Competence and confidence on the part of educators have increased, and educators, in turn, have developed instructional and technological advancements to successfully educate students with diverse needs within general education.

Over the past decades, case law (circuit and federal court rulings) has also clarified the intent of the law in favor of including all children. For example, the 1983 *Roncker v. Walter* case addressed the issue of "bringing educational services to the child" versus "bringing the child to the services." The case resolved in favor of integrated versus segregated placement, and it established a principle of portability. Thus, "if a desirable service currently provided in a segregated setting can feasibly be delivered in an integrated setting, it would be inappropriate under P.L. 94–142 [IDEA] to provide the service in a segregated environment" (700 F. 2d at 1063). In 1988, the U.S. Court of Appeals ruled in favor of Timothy W., a student considered "too disabled" by his school district to be entitled to an education. The ruling clarified the responsibility of school districts to educate all children and specified that the term *all* included in IDEA meant "all" children with disabilities—without exception.

In 1993, the U.S. Third Circuit Court of Appeals upheld the right of Rafael Oberti, a boy with Down syndrome, to receive his education in his neighborhood school with necessary supports, thereby placing the burden of proof for complying with IDEA's least-restrictive environment (LRE) requirements squarely on the school district and the state rather than the family (*Oberti v. Board of Education*, 1993). Likewise, in 1994, the Ninth Circuit Court of Appeals upheld the district court's decision in *Holland v. Sacramento Unified School District,* in which Judge Levi indicated that when school districts place students with disabilities, the presumption and starting point is the mainstream. More recently, in 2002, the Third Circuit Court of Appeals upheld the *Girty v. School District of Valley Grove* district court decision to continue the education of Charles "Spike" Girty, a student with moderate disabilities, in general education. The appeals court rejected the school district's contention that Spike needed a segregated placement because his educational level was significantly below that of his classmates and noted the following:

> The IDEA requires only that Spike be able to receive educational benefits when he is in the regular class, and that the benefits he receives when in the regular class with supplementary aids and services not be far outweighed by the benefits he would receive

in a self-contained segregated setting. . . . States and school districts are not asked to determine whether LRE is an appropriate policy but rather to determine how a child can be educated in the LRE. (*Girty v. School District of Valley Grove*, p. 14)

It is noteworthy that the U.S. Departments of Justice and Education filed amicus briefs in both the Holland and Girty cases, arguing in favor of educating both Rachael Holland and Spike Girty in general education classrooms with supplemental supports, aids, and services.

For some people, the rationale for embracing inclusive education is based on logical, practical, and legal considerations. Their question is, if it is possible to provide an integrated education with appropriate supports and services, if children with disabilities do have legal rights to education in regular education and courts are interpreting laws to favor inclusive options, and if families of children with disabilities are likely to accelerate their advocacy for inclusion based upon awareness of the negative outcomes of segregated education and favorable court decisions, why not spend educators' limited time, energy, and money on collaborative efforts to create successful integrated education experiences for all children rather than continue in conflict?

Procedural Issues

Few educators would disagree that paperwork dominates special education. Nationally, special educators devote an estimated 35 to 50 percent of their time to assessment and other documentation related to students' individualized education programs (IEPs) (Vermont Department of Education, 1990). Unfortunately, much of the assessment is conducted to comply with legal requirements to label and categorize students rather than to gather diagnostic information that assists instruction. Furthermore, an extensive examination of evaluation reports revealed that assessment results can be no more accurate than the flip of a coin (Ysseldyke et al., 1983). Even if labels were consistently valid and reliable, no evidence suggests that all children given a particular global label (e.g., autism, Down syndrome, emotional disorder, learning disability, multiple disabilities, or talented and gifted) will learn in the same way, are motivated by the same things, or have the same gifts or challenges.

The huge amount of special education paperwork—including required timelines, notices of meetings, timely development of educational goals and comprehensive reports, and annual review of IEPs—is, in fact, merely a procedural "proxy" measure of actual student change. For some—particularly special educators, parents, and advocates—procedural and financial issues such as the ones raised in this chapter spurred them to call for change in an educational system that labels and segregates a vast number of our children on the basis of educationally questionable assessment instruments and student monitoring procedures.

Population Increases

A major concern—particularly for special educators who must assess and serve students identified as having disabilities—is the rising number of children eligible for special education. A recent 13-year period saw a 23 percent increase in eligibility (Fuchs & Fuchs, 1994) and a 119 percent increase in those labeled "learning disabled" (Lipsky & Gartner, 1989). Such staggering and continuing annual rises are so out of hand that one state department of education projected that "nearly 50 percent of our students receive services from or are eligible for a variety of special programs serving students with disabilities, economic or social disadvantages, special talents, etc." (Vermont Department of Education, 1993, p. 1). That phenomenon causes some concerned citizens to ask, "Is the disability in the child, or is the disability somehow in the educational systems that we have created?"

Disjointed Incrementalism

As noted in Chapter 2, there has been much discussion about the dual systems of general and special education. In reality, we have not a dual system but a multiple system of education. Aside from general and special education, we have gifted education, vocational education, English-as-a-second-language education, at-risk education, alternative education, and so on. All are well intended, but they were launched separately in a disjointed and incremental fashion and are delivered separately in what could be referred to as an "egg carton" service delivery model. Each system or program has its own eligibility criteria, funding formulas, and advocacy groups that sometimes conflict with another's and, at the very least, lead to wasted resources because of poor coordination and duplication of services, personnel, materials, equipment, and accounting. That so many "special" programs have been created for so many children suggests we need a unified system of education to pull together the disjointed programs, resources, adults, and children.

Funding

Costs associated with segregating children can be significant in both human terms and dollars. When inclusive schooling was first proposed in the early 1980s, the anticipated cost of educating children with disabilities in local general education was an argument for why inclusion would not be possible. Since then, communities across the country have demonstrated that educating all children in local general education classrooms does not necessarily cost more. In some cases, reducing separate busing costs and eliminating duplicate services have saved dollars that could then be used to increase instructional resources, thus benefiting many children.

Interestingly, some opponents of inclusion have criticized the citing of potential cost savings of returning children "home" as inappropriate and unethical. Granted, inclusion should not be promoted for financial reasons alone; what is best for children is the ultimate rationale for a practice. However, nothing is wrong with being fiscally responsible. As noted previously, education has often squandered its resources through poor coordination among programs, service providers, and advocacy efforts. Most communities are experiencing cutbacks in education and clearly cannot afford anything less than efficient delivery of supports to children.

Philosophy

For some people, the most compelling rationale for embracing inclusive education is philosophical in nature: a belief that exclusion of any subgroup is a simple violation of civil rights and the principle of equal citizenship. They see a parallel between the struggle to include students with disabilities and the struggle for human and civil rights in the 1950s and 1960s, when officials blocked white schoolhouse doors to keep out African American children. They agree with statements by Chief Justice Earl Warren (1954) in the landmark *Brown v. Board of Education* decision that separateness in education can

> generate a feeling of inferiority as to [children's] status in the community that may affect their hearts and minds in a way unlikely ever to be undone. This sense of inferiority . . . affects the motivation of a child to learn . . . [and] has a tendency to retard . . . educational and mental development. (p. 493)

Those people know that the number-one determinant of the extent to which a child with disabilities has access to regular education is *where* the child's family happens to live. They see how arbitrary and unfair the determinant is. Accordingly, to create a society in which all people are valued, we must model that society in our schooling.

Demonstrations and Recognition

> More is learned from a single success than from multiple failures. A single success proves it can be done—whatever is, is possible.
>
> —G. J. Klopf (1979, p. 40)

As reported in Chapter 2, schools in every U.S. state have restructured for diversity and are implementing inclusive practices (Webb, 1994) to educate an increasingly diverse student body—including students with disabilities—in local general education classrooms. Inclusive education is a worldwide movement, not limited to the United States. At the 1994 United Nations world conference on special education in Salamanca, Spain, 92 nations signed the Salamanca Statement, which in part states:

> Education for children with special needs should be provided within the general education system, which has the best potential to combat discriminatory attitudes, create welcoming communities, and build an inclusive society. (UNESCO, 1994)

Clearly, all people benefit from having examples to observe, learn from, and imitate. Some people, however, need successful demonstrations to convince them that a practice—such as inclusive schooling—is possible and should be considered. In other words, demonstrations change the line of questioning from "Can such a thing be done?" to "How can we learn from the examples and make it work in our unique community?"

Mounting momentum and international support for inclusive educational practices can additionally influence people who think, "If these leaders and a mass of people consider inclusion a viable and valuable path to take, perhaps we should consider it for our community." Observers might be influenced by the support of leading national general educational organizations that have studied and written position papers to support policies and practices for actualizing inclusive schooling (see Chapter 2). They also might be influenced by support data from both special and regular educators. For example, in a multistate study of 680 education professionals who were experienced with inclusive practices, both regular and special education professionals favored teaching children with disabilities in general education using a shared collaborative relationship between general and special educators. Both groups perceived benefits for educators and children (Villa, Thousand, Meyers & Nevin, 1994). The study substantiates the positive findings of other research reviewed in Chapter 2.

Which Rationale Is Most Compelling for You?

Figure 3.3 offers a concept map of the 10 rationales for change presented in this chapter. We invite you to examine the figure and to reread sections of the chapter to clarify any rationales.

Figure 3.3

Rationales for Change

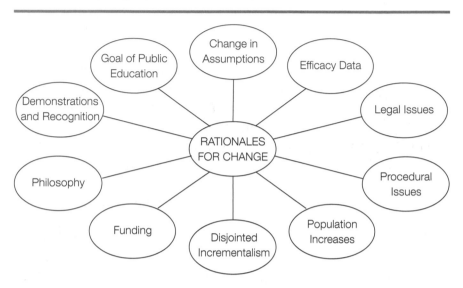

We then invite you to respond to the following questions:

1. Personally and professionally, which of the rationales are the most compelling to you? That is, which are most likely to lead you to reject segregation of general and special education and, instead, to support a unified, inclusive educational system?
2. Which of the rationales would your colleagues, supervisors, students, community members, and policymakers find most compelling?

Your answers to these two questions are important to the discussion in Chapter 4 on how beliefs and attitudes can be influenced to support inclusive education.

References

Baker, E., Wang, M., & Walberg, H. (1994). The effects of inclusion on learning. *Educational Leadership, 52*(4), 33–35.

Cole, D. A., & Meyer, L. H. (1991). Social integration and severe disabilities: A longitudinal analysis of child outcomes. *The Journal of Special Education, 25,* 340–351.

Costello, C. (1991). *A comparison of student cognitive and social achievement for handicapped and regular education students who are educated in integrated versus a substantially separate classroom.* Unpublished doctoral dissertation, University of Massachusetts, Amherst.

Freeman, S., & Alkin, M. (2000). Academic and social attainments of children with mental retardation in general education and special education settings. *Remedial and Special Education, 21*(1), 3–18.

Fuchs, D., & Fuchs, L. S. (1994). Inclusive schools movement and the radicalization of special education reform. *Exceptional Children, 60,* 294–309.

Ginott, H. (1972). *Teacher and child.* New York: Macmillan.

Girty v. School District of Valley Grove, No. 01-3934. (3rd Cir. 2002).

Glasser, W. (1986). *Control theory in the classroom.* New York: Harper and Row.

Hollowood, T., Salisbury, C., Rainforth, B., & Palombaro, M. (1994). Use of instructional time in classrooms serving students with and without severe disabilities. *Exceptional Children, 61*(3), 242–253.

Individuals with Disabilities Education Act (IDEA) of 1997, 20 U.S.C. § 1400(c)(5).

Kelly, D. (1992). Introduction. In T. Neary, A. Halvorsen, R. Kronberg, & D. Kelly (Eds.), *Curricular adaptations for inclusive classrooms* (pp. 1–6). San Francisco: California Research Institute for the Integration of Students with Severe Disabilities, San Francisco State University.

Klopf, G. J. (1979). *The principal and staff development in the school—with a special focus on the role of the principal in mainstreaming.* New York: Bank Street College of Education.

Kunc, N. (2000). Rediscovering the right to belong. In R. A. Villa & J. S. Thousand (Eds.), *Restructuring for caring and effective education: Piecing the puzzle together* (2nd ed., pp. 77–92). Baltimore: Paul H. Brookes.

Lipsky, D., & Gartner, A. (1989). *Beyond separate education: Quality education for all.* Baltimore: Paul H. Brookes.

Malsow, A. (1970). *Motivation and personality.* New York: Harper & Row

National Association of State Boards of Education (NASBE) Study Group on Special Education (1992, October). *Winners all: A call for inclusive schools.* Alexandria, VA: Author.

Oberti v. Board of Education, 995 F. 2nd 1204 (3rd Cir. 1993).

Roncker v. Walter, 700 F.2d 1058, l063 (6th Cir. 1983) cert. denied, 464 U.S. 864.

Scherer, M. (1992, December/1993, January). On savage inequalities: A conversation with Jonathan Kozol. *Educational Leadership, 50*(4), 4–9.

Sharpe, M. N., York, J. L., & Knight, J. (1994). Effects of inclusion on the academic performance of classmates without disabilities. *Remedial and Special Education, 15*(5), 281–287.

Strain, P. (1983). Generalization of autistic children's social behavior change: Effects of developmentally integrated and segregated settings. *Analysis and Intervention in Developmental Disabilities, 3*, 23–34.

Straub, D., & Peck, C. (1994). What are the outcomes for nondisabled students? *Educational Leadership, 52*(4), 36–40.

UNESCO. (1994). The Salamanca statement and framework for action on special education.

U.S. Department of Education. (1995). *Seventeenth annual report to Congress on the implementation of the Individuals with Disabilities Education Act.* Washington, DC: Author.

Van Bockern, S. L., Brendtro, L. K., & Brokenleg, M. (2000). Reclaiming our youth. In R. A. Villa & J. S. Thousand (Eds.), *Restructuring for caring and effective education: Piecing the puzzle together* (2nd ed., pp. 56–76). Baltimore: Paul H. Brookes.

Vermont Department of Education. (1990). *Report of the special commission on special education state of Vermont.* Montpelier, VT: Vermont Department of Education.

Vermont Department of Education. (1993, February). *Vermont Act 230 three years later: A report of the impact of Act 230;* Champaign, IL: University of Illinois.

Villa, R. A., Thousand, J. S., Meyers, H., & Nevin, A. I. (1994). *Regular and special education teacher and administrator perceptions of heterogeneous education.* Manuscript submitted for publication.

Warren, E. (1954). Brown v. Board of Education of Topeka, 347 U.S. 483, 493.

Webb, N. (1994). Special education: With new court decisions backing them, advocates see inclusion as a question of values. *The Harvard Education Letter* (4), 1–3. Cambridge, MA: Harvard University Press.

Ysseldyke, J., Thurlow, M., Graden, J., Wesson, C., Algozzine, B., & Deno, S. (1983). Generalizations from five years of research on assessment and decision-making. *Exceptional Education Quarterly, 4*, 79–93.

Chapter 4

Organizational Supports for Change Toward Inclusive Schooling

Jacqueline S. Thousand and Richard A. Villa

Why is change in organizations—schools included—so difficult and unwelcome, even with overwhelming evidence that the status quo does not work for many? Why do expectations for achieving excellence and equity for all children in our public schools seem beyond reach or ridiculous? Why do people in the midst of a change initiative feel confusion, anxiety, resistance, or frustration? Why does progress occur in some places and not in others? Why has teaching not achieved the desired results for many children?

Such questions have nagged us for years as we have promoted more inclusive educational options for children with disabilities. Somehow, we knew that there were understandable ways of leading organizations and people into and through change. But only after we had gone through and observed transformations of school cultures and practices did the answers begin to emerge. This chapter does not list absolute conclusions or prescriptions from "exemplary" schools that have succeeded in embracing inclusive education for the same reasons articulated by Margaret Wheatley (1994) in her assumption-shattering *Leadership and the New Science*:

> First, I no longer believe that [school] organizations can be changed by imposing a model developed elsewhere. So little transfers to, or even inspires, those trying to work at change in their own organizations. Second, . . . there is no objective reality out there waiting to reveal its secrets. There are no recipes

or formulae, no checklists or advice that describe "reality." There is only what we create through our engagement with others and with events. Nothing really transfers; everything is always new and different and unique to each of us. (p. 7)

We believe, as Wheatley does, that "we have only just begun the process of discovering and inventing the new organizational forms that will inhabit the 21st century" (1994, p. 5). That is, we are only beginning to explore paradigms of schooling that are inclusive and in accord with the predicted diversity and unpredictability of 21st-century life. As educational explorers and inventors of tomorrow, we must give up many if not all of our ideas of what did and did not work in school yesterday. Einstein understood the difficulty long ago, frequently observing that it is impossible to solve complex problems with the same consciousness we used to create them.

This chapter examines five variables—vision, skills, incentives, resources, and action planning—that contribute to the successful management of complex change in any organization. It concludes with insights into the change process.

Managing Complex Change

We are attracted to a model that comprises at least the five variables (vision, skills, incentives, resources, action planning) for predicting success or failure in managing complex change within an organization. We have noticed that if any one of the variables is unattended, the result is something other than the desired change (Knoster, Villa, & Thousand, 2000). This section describes the model:

- Build a *vision* of inclusive schooling within a community.
- Develop educators' *skills* and confidence to be inclusive educators.
- Create meaningful *incentives* for people to take the risk to embark on an inclusive schooling journey.
- Reorganize and expand human and other *resources* for teaching for and to diversity.

- Plan for and take *actions* devoted to strategies so people in schools see and get excited about a new big picture.

Building a Vision: Visionizing

According to Schlechty, "One of the greatest barriers to school reform is the lack of a clear and compelling vision" (1990, p. 137). Building a vision, or *visionizing,* is the first variable in the change formula. Unless we devote time and effort to building a common vision, the result may be confusion by some or many in the school and greater community.

We use the term *visionizing* (Parnes, 1988) to describe the desired outcome of the first change variable because an action verb suggests the active mental struggle and the "mental journey from the known to the unknown" (Hickman & Silva, 1984, p. 151) that people go through when they reconceptualize their beliefs and declare public ownership of a new view. Visionizing involves creating and communicating a compelling picture of a desired future state and inducing others to commit to that future.

Leaders of schools involved in inclusive education stress the importance of clarifying for themselves, school personnel, and the community a vision that is based on the assumptions that (1) *all* children are capable of learning, (2) *all* children have a right to an education with their peers in their community's schools, and (3) the school system is responsible for attempting to address the unique needs of *all* children in the community. To articulate such an inclusive vision is necessary. To adopt the vision is not sufficient. Visionizing requires fostering widespread understanding and consensus about the vision. The following sections address consensus building.

Examination of Rationales for Change

One strategy to build consensus is to educate people about the theoretical, ethical, and data-based rationales for inclusive education. (See Chapter 3 for discussion of the multiple rationales for change and the concept map of these rationales.) We asked two questions: (1) Which of the rationales are the most compelling for you (i.e., most likely to lead you to support a unified, inclusive educational system)? And (2) which of the rationales would your colleagues, supervisors, students, community members, and policymakers find most compelling? Your answers to these two questions are vitally important to visionizing the change process. Why?

Our experience tells us that to build consensus, different people find different rationales to be compelling, and each rationale is compelling to someone. Norm Kunc (personal communication, July 17, 2003) suggests that we picture each person as a circle with two halves. One half comprises a person's concerns about a proposed change, innovation, or new concept; the other half comprises the beliefs (supportive or nonsupportive) about the change. He further suggests that if we hope to shift a person's belief in favor of the change, we must first listen to and identify the person's concerns (i.e., questions, fears, nightmares, confusions) about the change.

In other words, as change agents, we must first solicit and listen to the concerns of everyone affected by a shift to inclusive schooling (teachers, parents, students, community members, school board). We must next use that information to determine which rationales speak to each individual's priority concerns. Fiscal and legal rationales may speak to administrators and school board members; disappointing efficacy data may speak to the parents of students with disabilities and the students themselves; proceduralism and the disjointed or incremental nature of special service systems may speak to special educators tired of isolation and endless hours of paperwork. We can then structure opportunities so we communicate the supporting information for rationales that are most compelling to those people. We may communicate in any number of ways: inservice training events, distribution of readings with follow-up discussions, and videotapes of or visitations to schools that have adopted inclusive visions and have successfully transformed. Finally, being knowledgeable about concerns allows us to seriously address them when planning or implementing processes by vigilantly asking, "How can we ensure that people's worst nightmares do not come true?"

Visionizing is really about replacing an old culture with a new one and managing the personal loss that cultural change inevitably stirs. New heroes and heroines, rituals and symbols, and histories must be constructed. New histories replace the old when traditional solutions (usually tacking on yet another program or professional when children with new differences arrive in school) and other educational inequities (the racial, ethnic, and economic discrimination that arises from tracking, special education, and gifted and talented programs) are loudly and publicly pointed out as ineffective, inefficient, and counter to the desired vision of inclusive learning opportunities. Of particular importance is introducing and expecting the use of new language and labels that are educative. For example, to value all children for their differences, we must use "person first" language (Cecilia, who happens to have Down syndrome; Juan, who is not yet proficient in English) rather than deficit-oriented language (that Down syndrome girl; the ESL kid). *heard this before*

Makes sense

Mission Statements

A second powerful strategy is to have representatives of school and community stakeholder groups examine the district's or school's current mission statement and reformulate a mission and objectives to support all students. Engaging people in participatory decision making about a vision or mission results in greater ownership of the resulting statement than when it is imposed on them. We caution people never to formulate separate mission statements for special versus general education, because they would simply perpetuate "dual system" thinking and action.

Clearly, risks are involved in turning over such an important function to people who, because of their diverse professional and personal perspectives, will initially differ in the degree to which they support inclusive education. That risk, however, can be minimized by ensuring that the committee has been informed of the ethical, theoretical, and data-based rationales for change (see Chapter 3) and that the committee has at least some members with an in-depth understanding of and commitment to inclusive education. Although clarifying and promoting an inclusive school philosophy in a mission statement is an important symbolic and guiding endeavor, we must recognize that a school community need not have a formal statement to alter organizational structures and instructional approaches that bar including all students.

Respect for What We Expect

Consensus can be fostered by respecting what we expect—encouraging, recognizing, and publicly acknowledging staff members and students who plunge in as early innovators and pioneers who model and actively promote inclusion. We should ask staff members and students what they consider rewarding. For example, public recognition would embarrass some people, but attending a conference on inclusion would be a treat. Furthermore, any person—bus driver, secretary, cafeteria worker, volunteer—should be a candidate for acknowledgment, because each person has the power through word or action to advance or impede a vision.

Visionizers

Who can or should initiate change? We suggest that anyone can be a visionizer or change agent. It is not important where on the organizational chart a person falls. What is important is that visionizers not only assist and nurture others through the change process but also steady themselves for the natural resistance that they will meet from some. They must acknowledge that change means cultural transformation (which can take many years), they must be patient, and they must not leave when times get tough.

Visionizers know that their job is to create cognitive dissonance, discomfort, chaos, and a sense of urgency and even rage in the school and community. Leadership by outrage and passion initiates change because, as other people observe and feel the outrage, the potential for outrage is kindled within themselves. "Outrage tells people what is important" (Sergiovanni, 1992, p. 74). So visionizers "talk up" the vision and supporting innovations and innovators, persuade people to adopt the vision, and coach them to perform their daily schoolwork in accordance with the vision. Although visionizers take every opportunity to build consensus, they know that no single teaching strategy or learning style is privileged; strategies will vary, reflecting the unique demographics, history, and current beliefs of each community. Finally, visionizers intuitively know that change is a very personal process and that the best way to get people to take a risk on the unfamiliar is to listen to their concerns; to believe in them; and to give them opportunities, training, and support to try.

Building Skills for Educators in an Inclusive School

A school system may have the vision, incentives, resources, and action plan to accomplish the desired change of becoming an inclusive school, but unless educators believe they have the skills to respond to students' and colleagues' needs, a likely outcome will be anxiety because they doubt they are good teachers. Clearly, the more diverse the students are, the more skilled the educators must be as a *collective* instructional body. We highlight *collective* to emphasize that educators in a school need not all have the same content and instructional skills, but they must readily access one another so they can share their skills across students and classrooms.

Areas of Common Training

No matter how exciting or promising an innovation seems, educators need training, guided practice, feedback, and opportunities to problem solve with colleagues. Further, for an innovation to become the new culture, people must understand how it will benefit their personal and professional growth, as well as the growth of their students (Hord, Rutherford, Huling-Austin, & Hall, 1987). For specific training content as you build teacher capacity, see Chapters 5 and 6 for exemplary curricular, instructional, and assessment practices to consider for an inservice agenda. We emphasize the importance of giving people training choices: courses, mentoring, team teaching, study groups, summer institutes, or workshop series.

Who Gets Training?

Anyone is a candidate for inservice training because anyone can resist or support inclusive education. Although initially training may be delivered only to innovators and early adopters, eventually everyone—teachers, administrators, paraprofessionals, related service personnel, secretarial and support staff, students, school board members, parents, community members—needs at least a common core of knowledge about the vision, rationale, and benefits of the innovation. To excuse the reluctant, resistant, or apathetic will divide people, foster factions and resentment toward nonparticipants, reinforce a this-too-will-pass mentality, and generally work against developing a unified new culture. Training in support of inclusive education never ends, because new staff members must learn the values and practices of inclusion. And people always need to be renewed through training so they can impart their skills to others and refine what they already do well.

Creating Incentives to Engage People in Inclusive Schooling

A school system can have a vision of change, personnel can have skills and abundant resources, and a plan of action can be set into motion. Yet without incentives that are meaningful to each person affected by the change, the outcome may be passive or active resistance rather than excited engagement. Schools successful in achieving a challenging mission have developed a common spirit of inspiring enthusiasm, devotion, and intense regard for the vision and honor of the group. Promoting esprit de corps requires structuring incentives according to the following steps:

- Be sure to attend to teams as well as individuals to highlight the importance of and pride in collaborative efforts.
- Spend time in the trenches with teachers and students learning what they are doing well so their accomplishments can be publicly and privately acknowledged.
- Ask staff members and students what *they* value as an incentive, because what is rewarding to one person may be of little significance to another.
- Overlook no one, because a bus driver or custodian can do as much to hasten the acceptance or demise of inclusive education as can an administrator or professional educator.

Ways to motivate people and to reinforce words and deeds that reflect the inclusive vision include the following:

- Send short notes of praise ("The peer tutors from your classroom are providing very effective instruction").

- Post thank-you letters from visitors.
- Offer special training opportunities to innovators.
- Ask innovators to serve as mentors for those new to inclusive practices.
- Ask teachers and students to tinker with and fine-tune innovations and to invent ways of doing things even better.
- Provide support for travel to conferences or other schools engaged in inclusive education.
- Host regular forums for airing concerns and generating viable solutions.
- Create and support opportunities to make presentations at conferences, school board meetings, parent–teacher organizations, and community gatherings.
- Structure off-campus retreats for collaborative planning efforts.

Although many incentives appeal to specific individuals, the one incentive that is common to and highly valued by everyone engaged in education and educational reform is time—time for shared reflection and planning with colleagues. As stated by Raywid, "The time necessary to examine, reflect on, amend, and redesign programs is not *auxiliary* to teaching responsibilities—nor is it 'released time' from them. It is absolutely central to such responsibilities, and essential to making school succeed (1993, p. 34)." Figure 4.1 lists ways that schools have attempted to meet the time challenge.

Although incentives are important ingredients in a change formula, heavy reliance on extrinsic incentives (e.g., honors, financial awards) can interfere with change. Sergiovanni (1990) explains:

> Traditional management theory is based on the principle "what gets rewarded gets done." . . . [Unfortunately,] when rewards can no longer be provided, the work no longer will be done. Work performance becomes contingent upon a bartering arrangement rather than being self-sustaining because of moral principle or a deeper psychological connection. A better strategy upon which to base our efforts is "what is rewarding gets done." When something is rewarding, it gets done even when "no one is looking." (p. 22)

Figure 4.1

Strategies for Expanding Time for Collaborative Planning,
Teaching, and Reflection

BORROWED TIME

1. Rearrange the school day to get a 50- to 60-minute block of time before or after school for coteachers to plan.
2. Lengthen the school day for students by 15 to 30 minutes on four days, allowing for early student dismissal on the fifth to gain a significant block of time (one to two hours) for coteachers to meet.

COMMON TIME

3. Ask coteachers to identify when during the day and week they prefer to plan; then redesign the master schedule to accommodate their preference with a block for common preparation.

TIERED TIME

4. Layer preparation time with existing functions such as lunch and recess.

RESCHEDULED TIME

5. Use staff development days for coteachers to do more long-range planning.
6. Use faculty meeting time to problem solve common coteaching issues of immediate or long-range importance.
7. Build at least one coteacher planning day into the school schedule each marking period or month.
8. Build in time for more intensive coteacher planning sessions by lengthening the school year for teachers (not students) or by shortening the school year for students (not teachers).

RELEASED TIME

9. Go to year-round schooling with three-week breaks every quarter; devote four or five days of each three-week intersession to coteacher planning as professional development days.

FREED-UP TIME

10. Institute a community service component to the curriculum; when students are in the community (e.g., Thursday afternoons), coteachers meet to plan.
11. Schedule "specials" (art, music, physical education), clubs, and tutorials during the same blocks (e.g., first and second periods) so that coteachers have at least that much extra time to plan.
12. Engage parents and community members in conducting half-day or full-day exploratory, craft, hobby (e.g., gourmet cooking, puppetry, photography), theater, or other experiential programs to free time for coteachers to plan.

Figure 4.1 (continued)

Strategies for Expanding Time for Collaborative Planning,
Teaching, and Reflection

13. Partner with colleges and universities; have their faculty teach in the school, provide demonstrations, or conduct university-campus experiences to free time for coteachers to plan.

PURCHASED TIME

14. Hire permanent substitutes to free coteachers for planning during the day rather than before or after school.
15. Compensate coteachers for spending vacation or holiday time on planning with either pay or comp time during noninstructional school-year days.

FOUND TIME

16. Strategically use serendipitous times that occasionally occur (e.g., snow days, student assemblies) to plan.

NEW TIME

17. In what ways might the school administration provide coteachers with incentives that would motivate them to use their own time to plan?

Alternatives to extrinsic rewards are intrinsic rewards, which people respond to "because of obligations, duties, a sense of righteousness, felt commitments, and other reasons with moral overtones ... [or because of] finding what they are doing to be personally significant in its own right" (Sergiovanni, 1992, p. 58). Intrinsic motivation includes recognizing one's increased effectiveness as evidenced by (1) student development and happiness, (2) pride in one's professional risk taking and growth and the accompanying recognition from respected colleagues and students, (3) personal satisfaction, or (4) the experience of *flow*. Csikszentmihalyi describes flow as "the state in which people are so involved in an activity that nothing else seems to matter; the experience itself is so enjoyable that people will do it even at great cost, for the sheer sake of doing it" (1990, p. 4). We have learned that genuine and sustainable changes in culture and dedication to inclusive schooling depend on people who become motivated by their emotions, values, beliefs, and social bonds with colleagues rather than by outside forces.

Gathering Resources for Inclusive Education

A school system may comprise people who have a common vision, technical skills in instruction and assessment, incentives, and a sensible plan of action for change. But unless those people feel that they have the needed resources to do the job, they will likely experience frustration that can zap their energy and enthusiasm and can draw them away from their change efforts. Resources in education may be technical and material (e.g., paper and pencils, computer hardware and software, curriculum materials, and concepts) or organizational (i.e., how the school day, week, and year and the people in the organization are arranged) in nature. Time is an example of an organizational resource (and incentive) in great shortage in many schools. The human resource—the relationships with other adults and children and their unique gifts, talents, and trades—is the most important to school health and improvement. Support from colleagues, students, formal leaders, and others in the community often is what people are really crying for when they are frustrated and need resources.

Role Redefinition to Access Adult Resources

Teaching has been characterized as a "lonely profession" (Sarason, Levine, Godenberg, Cherlin, & Bennet, 1966, p. 74). Teachers get the message that they are alone from various sources: (1) teacher preparation programs (e.g., solo versus collaborative teaching as the culminating practicum event or distinct general versus special education programs), (2) organization of schools into separate classrooms headed by one teacher for many students, and (3) job descriptions and teacher evaluation procedures that emphasize individual rather than collaborative performance. The absurdity of teaching in isolation is obvious. Yet the norms, traditions, and organizational structure of many schools perpetuate the segregation of staff members and students, as well as the somewhat standard and inflexible expectations of the roles of people with different labels (e.g., administrators, teachers, paraeducators, specialists of all sorts, parents).

For educators to readily access the resources of other educational personnel, everyone in the school system must relinquish traditional roles, drop distinct professional labels, and redistribute their job functions across any number of other people. Figure 4.2 shows how job functions can and have changed in schools that meld human resources through dramatic, systemwide role redefinition. Flexibility and fluidity are the main aim of role redefinition. Exactly who does what from one year to the next should always be subject to change and determined by students' needs and the complementary skills (and needs) of the educators distributing job functions among themselves. Job titles and formal definitions determine the way that people behave. Thus, to further signal a change in culture, we should formulate new policies and job descriptions that expect, inspect, and respect a collaborative ethic.

Team Teaching to Merge Resources

With shifting and more fluid job functions comes the opportunity to rearrange school personnel in various collaborative relationships: (1) mentoring and peer coaching teams, (2) peer buddy systems that pair newly hired teachers with veteran teachers, and (3) teaching teams— an organizational and instructional arrangement of two or more members of the school and greater community who distribute among themselves the planning, instructional, and evaluation responsibilities for the same students regularly for an extended time. By jigsawing unique instructional expertise, areas of curriculum background, and personal interests of formerly isolated regular and specialized educational personnel, teaching teams bring a richer learning experience to all students, as well as a higher teacher-to-student ratio, enhanced problem-solving capacity, and more immediate and accurate diagnosis of student needs and delivery of appropriate instruction (Thousand & Villa, 2000).

Administrator's Role as a Resource

School administrators are a critical resource for teachers, as Littrell, Billingsley, and Cross (1994) discovered when they examined the

Figure 4.2

Changes in Job Responsibilities of School Personnel
Before and After Role Redefinition

Role	Traditional Responsibilities	Redefined Responsibilities
General Education Administrator	Exercises responsibility for managing general education program	Exercises responsibility for managing educational programs for all students
	Places special programs within general education facilities, but recognizes that program responsibility belongs to special education rather than general education administrators	Articulates the vision and provides emotional support to staff members as they experience the change process
		Participates as a member of collaborative problem-solving teams that invent solutions to barriers inhibiting the successful inclusion and education of any child
		Secures supports to enable staff members to meet the needs of all children
General Educator	Refers students who do not "fit" into the traditional program for diagnosis, remediation, and possible removal	Shares responsibility with special educators and other support personnel for teaching all assigned children
	Teaches children who "fit" within the standard curriculum	Seeks aid of special educators and other support personnel for students experiencing difficulty in learning
		Collaboratively plans and teaches with other members of the staff and community to meet the needs of all learners
		Recruits and trains students to be tutors and peer buddies for other students

Figure 4.2 (continued)

Changes in Job Responsibilities of School Personnel
Before and After Role Redefinition

Role	Traditional Responsibilities	Redefined Responsibilities
Special Educator	Provides instruction to students eligible for services in resource rooms, special classes, and special schools	Collaborates with general educators and other support personnel to meet the needs of all learners Team teaches with regular educators in general education classes Recruits and trains students to be peer tutors and peer buddies for other students
Psychologist	Tests, diagnoses, assigns labels, and determines eligibility for students' admission to special programs	Collaborates with teachers to define problems Creatively designs interventions Team teaches Provides social skills training to classes of students Conducts authentic assessments Trains students to be conflict mediators, peer tutors, and buddies for one another Offers counseling to students

Figure 4.2 (continued)

Changes in Job Responsibilities of School Personnel
Before and After Role Redefinition

Role	Traditional Responsibilities	Redefined Responsibilities
Support Staff Member (e.g., social worker, speech and language pathologist, physical therapist)	Diagnoses, labels, and provides direct services to students in settings other than the classroom Provides support only to students eligible for a particular special program	Assesses and provides direct services to students within general education classrooms and community settings Supports students not eligible for special education Trains classroom teachers, instructional assistants, volunteers, and students to carry out support services Shares responsibility to meet the needs of all students
Paraeducator (teaching assistant)	Works in segregated programs If working in general education classrooms, stays in proximity of and works only with student(s) eligible for special services	Provides services to a variety of students in general education settings Facilitates natural peer support within general education settings
Student	Primarily works independently and competes with other students for "best" performance Is a passive recipient of learning	Often works with other students in cooperative learning arrangements Is actively involved in instruction, advocacy, and decision making for self and other students

effects of principal support on special and general educators' stress, job satisfaction, school commitment, health, and intent to stay in teaching. Emotional support—showing teachers that they are esteemed and worthy of concern through "open communication, showing appreciation, taking an interest in teachers' work, and considering teachers' ideas" (p. 297)—emerged as the most important support provided by administrators.

Administrators assist with reorganizing teachers' lives through a flexible and responsive master schedule, thus enabling teachers to meet and teach as teams. To build a coordinated master schedule, administrators must first ask teachers to identify the various peer collaborations that they are currently involved in or that they would like to structure. They must mesh the planning and meeting needs of collaborative teams with schoolwide functions such as faculty meetings, curriculum development meetings, and inservice training events. Administrators can work with teachers and the community to modify the master schedule to create more time (in ways identified in Figure 4.1) for adult face-to-face interaction and meaningful incentives that advance inclusive education.

Students as Resources

The terms *teaming* and *collaboration* usually conjure up images of adults joining forces. However, schools attempting inclusive education have discovered the importance of expanding potential collaborators to include students and the importance of practicing what they preach about collaboration by sharing their instructional and decision-making power with students in a climate of mutual respect. Among the limitless collaborations that benefit students and educators alike are (1) students as instructors in partner learning, cooperative group learning, and adult–student teaching teams (see Chapter 5); (2) students sitting on planning teams for their own and classmates' Individualized Education Programs (IEPs) to advocate for their own or friends' interests; and (3) students sharing decision-making responsibility by serving on curriculum and discipline committees or the school board.

Outside Partnerships

Developing partnerships with state department personnel, faculty of institutions of higher education, and individuals in other school districts with a similar interest in inclusive education can gain much-needed human, political, and fiscal resources. State Department of Education personnel may provide fiscal incentives or regulatory relief for innovations. They may also provide valuable public relations support for inclusive schooling through circulars, publications, and public presentations. Collaboration by higher education and school districts offers mutual benefits to both organizations. Together, they can design and solicit state or federal support for model demonstrations; arrange for valuable internship experiences for students in teacher preparation programs; conduct research to document the challenges, solutions, and effects of inclusive schooling practices; or codevelop and deliver coursework to foster new roles or skills necessary for inclusive educational practice. Finally, schools sharing a common vision of inclusive education should share or exchange resources, including personnel (e.g., reciprocal inservice presenters, a specialist in nonverbal communication); jointly address barriers to change; form coalitions to advocate for change in outdated teacher preparation programs and state-level funding formulas and policies; and celebrate their successes with one another.

Planning and Taking Action

Action planning is the last of the five variables for promoting complex change. Individuals within a system may have the vision, skills, incentives, and resources for change. Without coordinated planning for action, however, the experience may be like running on a treadmill, expending energy getting nowhere. Action planning requires participants to be thoughtful and communicative about the process of change (i.e., how, with whom, and in what sequence the steps or stages of change are formulated, communicated, and set into motion). Action plans are tricky because they require the right mix of planning versus action and the continual involvement of the many people affected by the change.

The Right Mix Without Overplanning

Alex Osborn (1993), a pioneer in the field of creativity, was noted for saying that a fair idea put into action was much better than a good idea left on the polishing wheel. He recognized that it is possible to plan something to death. Unless planning quickly leads to action, interest will wane, which Schlechty (1990) acknowledged when he suggested that we take a "ready, fire, aim" (rather than "ready, aim, fire") approach to planning change initiatives. Furthermore, people must be comfortable with the unknown and go with the flow. Throughout the change process, they must accept how long change may take, what steps must be taken, and how things must be adjusted and readjusted.

Principles of Systematic Planning

Having stated the caveats to be flexible and to resist the urge to overplan, we urge school districts initiating inclusive education not to make the mistake that some have made by not planning. Action plans for change can take many forms and may use any number of decision-making processes. One popular decision-making process— strategy planning—offers several guiding principles for moving people from a somewhat ethereal vision to concrete action (Cook, 1990; Kaufman, 1991). We have found the following principles to be particularly useful:

- *Do not plan in a vacuum; look outside.* Knowing information about social, political, cultural, and economic trends external to the education world is critical. Pay close attention to as much of this information as possible.
- *Look inside.* The school system already has resources and strengths, as well as barriers to successful education. Carefully examine and discover the current internal strengths and nonstrengths of the school system's policies, practices, organizational structures, and so forth.
- *Include stakeholders in decision making.* Be as participative as possible in decision making. Be sure all relevant stakeholder groups are represented in the planning process and are communicated with regularly. People are at the core of change; we cause or impede it.

- *Monitor the change.* Change is dynamic. The forces that drive and restrain change tend to shift over time, and the outcome of actions taken is unpredictable. Therefore, meet regularly to review progress, revise and modify plans, disband groups that have accomplished their tasks, and create new ad hoc teams to develop action plans for additional strategies.
- *Revisit the vision.* The vision can get lost or distorted over time. New people come into the school system and community who may be unaware of or misunderstand the vision. Keep people on track by periodically re-examining the vision and using the media (e.g., school newsletters, TV spots, the school district's Web page, newspaper articles) to educate the public.
- *Put things in writing.* People do best if their decisions are put into a systematic written format (action plan) that specifies in detail who will do what by when and to what criterion.

Involvement and Communication

Engaging people in action planning for a change that will affect them is important in helping them develop ownership for the coming changes and believing that change really *will* occur. Planning is the alarm signaling to everyone that things will no longer be the same. However, for planning to accomplish that end, visionizers must effectively communicate the desired future and must get people to see clearly how it can be achieved and what part each person will play. Sometimes visionizers with the strongest sense of purpose and brilliant intuitions about what needs to be done can't help people see how change will take place. They end up imposing strategies and appearing authoritarian not because they wish to, but "because only they see the decisions that need to be made. Leaders . . . [must] have the ability to conceptualize their strategic insights so that they become public knowledge, open to challenge and further improvement" (Senge, 1990, p. 356).

Healthy Assumptions

In healthy organizations, people examine their unconscious assumptions about how the organization operates. In a healthy systems change effort, people are advised to do the same. Change facilitators engaged in action planning are advised to adopt the healthy assumptions that (1) their version of change is not necessarily the one that will or should result; (2) no amount of knowledge ever clarifies which action is the "correct" one to take; (3) manageability is achieved by thinking big and starting small; (4) lack of participation or commitment is not necessarily a rejection of the vision—other factors (e.g., insufficient skills, incentives, resources) may be the cause; (5) changing culture, not installing an innovation, is the real agenda; and (6) any action plan must be based on the five previous assumptions (Fullan & Stiegelbauer, 1991).

Evaluation of Concerns

Regular and continuous evaluation is an integral part of action planning. What is worthy of evaluation? Clearly, we want to know if educating children with disabilities in general education is working. Are students with and without disabilities achieving academic success and experiencing elements of the *Circle of Courage* (Van Bockern, Brendtro, & Brokenleg, 2000), that is, belonging, mastery, independence, and generosity? What are postschool outcomes (e.g., employment, continuing education, civic contributions)? We also want to know about affective and process variables such as educators' feelings at various points during the change process and their stages of concern (e.g., from little involvement, to informational or personal concerns, to management or refinement concerns) (Hall & Hord, 1987). Both outcome and affective or process evaluations offer change agents the information that they need to adjust the action plan or to undertake new actions to deal with concerns, failures, confusions, and successes.

Any question that is important enough for a stakeholder to pose is worthy of answering (evaluating). The evaluation agenda should be as flexible and open as the planning process. Sometimes quite unexpected outcomes occur. For example, a friend of the authors experienced a 25-point increase in her tested IQ following two years of full inclusion in her local high school (J. Pauley, personal communication, October 17, 2003). The lesson is that everyone needs to keep an eye out for the unexpected and to act as action researchers who note and talk about what they experience in school on a day-to-day basis.

Summary and Final Thoughts

We now think we know enough about change so the transition to inclusive schooling no longer seems impossible. We know, for example, that schools are cultures and that to actualize a new vision, a new culture must replace the old. We know that change inevitably creates cognitive and interpersonal conflict that can be managed through creative problem solving. We know fundamental change occurs when the roles, rules, relationships, and responsibilities of everyone (students included) are redefined. Hierarchical power relationships must be altered so everyone affected by impending change has a voice and role in decision making. We know that change is not necessarily progress; only close attention to valued outcomes will tell us if change equals progress. We know that action planning is important and that resources, incentives, and skill building make a difference. We know (1) that commitment to a change often does not occur until people have developed skills and gained experience with the change (McLaughlin, 1991) and (2) that initial negative or neutral feelings toward inclusion can and do change.

Clearly, the complex nature of re-engineering can be difficult. Yet an increasing number of communities have taken the plunge and implemented a vision of inclusive education with integrity and quality. Choice is a key word, here, as Senge (1990) points out:

> Choice is different [from] desire. Try an experiment. Say, "I want." Now, say, "I choose." What is the difference? For most people, "I want" is passive; "choose" is active. For most, wanting is a state of deficiency—we want what we do not have. Choosing is a state of sufficiency—we have what we truly want. As most of us look back over our life, we can see that certain choices we made played a pivotal role in how our life developed. So, too, will the choices we make in the future. (p. 360)

Effective inclusive school organizations can be and are crafted by individuals who activate what is known about change processes that steward a larger vision.

References

Cook, B. (1990). *Bill Cook's strategic planning in America's schools.* Rosslyn, VA: American Association of School Administrators.

Csikszentmihalyi, M. (1990). *Flow: The psychology of optimal experience.* New York: HarperCollins.

Fullan, M. G., & Stiegelbauer, S. (1991). *The new meaning of educational change* (2nd ed.). New York: Teachers College Press.

Hall, G. E., & Hord, S. (1987). *Change in schools: Facilitating the process.* Albany, NY: State University of New York Press.

Hickman, C., & Silva, M. (1984). *Creating excellence: Managing corporate culture, strategy, and change in the new age.* New York: New American Library.

Hord, S., Rutherford, W., Huling-Austin, L., & Hall, G. (1987). *Taking charge of change.* Alexandria, VA: Association for Supervision and Curriculum Development.

Kaufman, R. (1991). *Strategic planning plus: An organizational guide.* Glenview, IL: Scott, Foresman.

Knoster, T., Villa, R., & Thousand, J. (2000). A framework for thinking about systems change. In R. Villa and J. Thousand (Eds.) *Restructuring for caring and effective education: Piecing the puzzle together* (2nd edition). Baltimore: Paul H. Brookes.

Littrell, P. C., Billingsley, B. S., & Cross, L. H. (1994). The effects of principal support on special and general educators' stress, job satisfaction, school commitment, health, and intent to stay in teaching. *Remedial and Special Education, 15*, 297–310.

McLaughlin, M. V. (1991). In A. R. Oden (Ed.), *Education policy implementation* (pp. 143–156). Albany, NY: State University of New York Press.

Osborn, A. (1993). *Applied imagination: Principles and procedures of creative problem solving* (3rd rev. ed.). Buffalo, NY: Creative Education Foundation Press.

Parnes, S. J. (1988). *Visionizing: State-of-the-art processes for encouraging innovative excellence.* East Aurora, NY: D.O.K. Publishers.

Raywid, M. A. (1993). Finding time for collaboration. *Educational Leadership, 51*(1), 30–34.

Sarason, S., Levine, M., Godenberg, I., Cherlin, D., & Bennet, E. (1966). *Psychology in community settings: Clinical, educational, vocational and social aspects.* New York: John Wiley and Sons.

Schlechty, P. (1990). *Schools for the 21st century: Leadership imperatives for educational reform.* San Francisco: Jossey-Bass.

Senge, P. (1990). *The fifth discipline: The art and practice of the learning organization.* New York: Doubleday.

Sergiovanni, T. J. (1990). *Value-added leadership: How to get extraordinary performance in schools.* Orlando, FL: Harcourt Brace Jovanovich.

Sergiovanni, T. J. (1992). *Moral leadership: Getting to the heart of school improvement.* San Francisco: Jossey-Bass.

Thousand, J. S., & Villa, R. A. (2000). Collaborative teaming: A powerful tool in school restructuring. In R. A. Villa & J. S. Thousand (Eds.), *Restructuring for caring and effective education: Piecing the puzzle together* (pp. 254–291). Baltimore: Paul H. Brookes.

Van Bockern, S., Brendtro, L., & Brokenleg, M. (2000). Reclaiming our youth. In R. A. Villa & J. S. Thousand (Eds.), *Restructuring for caring and effective education: Piecing the puzzle together* (pp. 56–76). Baltimore: Paul H. Brookes.

Wheatley, M. J. (1994). *Leadership and the new science: Learning about organization from an orderly universe.* San Francisco: Berrett-Koehler Publishers.

Changing Views from the Porch: Second-Generation Inclusion at Cook Hill School

Joanne Godek, Katharine Shepherd Furney, and Mary Lynn Riggs

Cook Hill Elementary School (pseudonym for an urban Vermont elementary school), like other schools across the United States, has practiced elements of an inclusive educational model since the mid-1980s. Cook Hill has approximately 350 students in kindergarten through 5th grade. The following story traces the school's recent efforts to restructure and promote a "second-generation" inclusion approach of supporting *all* students in general education (Thousand & Villa, 2000). We hope our story provides direction for other schools wishing to follow a similar path.

Getting Started: The Change Process

On an idyllic summer evening in Vermont, a group of us sat on the porch of our principal's farmhouse and discussed how we might change the service delivery model at our school. With chart paper, markers, and questions in hand, we brainstormed how we could best meet the needs of all learners. We had already worked to ensure that all students in our elementary school were included in general education classrooms. Our new task was to improve the quality of our services and to create a more proactive and flexible model for meeting a greater range of student needs. As we talked, we wondered, "What could we do to support students who were not meeting standards, yet were not

identified with a disability? How could we ensure that students
with the most challenging learning needs are getting good diag-
nostic instruction? How could we . . . ?"

The conversation that began five summers ago was prompted by challenges related to the school's initial efforts to serve students with disabilities in general education classrooms. Special education, Title I, and
remedial reading services were available to meet a range of student
needs, but classroom teachers, as well as specialists, still worked in
parallel systems that afforded few opportunities to exchange ideas
or integrate services. Special education paraprofessionals were perceived as having too much responsibility for working with children
with intensive needs and too little contact with their appointed special education supervisors. Many believed that a less categorical
system would be more flexible in its use of staff and resources. Such
a system could usher in a second generation of inclusion.

The formal change process began when concerned teachers
and the principal invited a representative group of the school community to the principal's home for uninterrupted planning time. In
retrospect, many saw the conversation as a turning point in the life
of the school because of a few key factors. First, the school established a collective vision for *all* children built around the *Circle of
Courage* framework (see Chapter 3), which emphasized the need for
a sense of belonging, mastery, independence, and generosity among
all students (Brendtro, Brokenleg, & Van Bockern, 1997). The vision
was well suited to the school's established culture; it validated a
long-standing focus on achievement while acknowledging the
equally important need to address students' social, affective, and
emotional development.

Second, the principal's porch cohort understood that some
people preferred to begin the change process by discussing "big picture" issues while others preferred to move quickly to develop and
implement concrete plans of action. Thus, discussions addressed
how this *Circle of Courage* could be translated into concrete actions,
as well as changes in roles, relationships, and organizational structures within the school.

Third, the principal's recognition of the interplay between "top-down" and "bottom-up" approaches to leadership facilitated the school's change process. As the school's formal leader, the principal is viewed as a skilled facilitator. Figure A summarizes the advice that the principal gave during the school's transformation toward second-generation inclusion. She acted as a change agent, helping to shape a vision and procuring resources for implementing plans. She also worked diligently to cultivate bottom-up, shared leadership empowerment throughout the school because she knew that staff members who were actively engaged in change would earn intrinsic rewards as they developed new skills, formed deeper collegial relationships, and experienced greater satisfaction in their work.

Making a Difference: Snapshots of Change

Stephanie, the speech and language pathologist, arrives at the elementary school early. She is excited because two 1st grade teachers have invited her into their classrooms. Together, Stephanie and the two teachers plan and deliver a literacy program that is diagnostic and effective for all 1st graders. Stephanie used to serve all students who were eligible for speech, language, or articulation services. Now she is part of the kindergarten/grade 1 team known as the "K/1 House," which focuses on intensive literacy and language instruction that all young learners need.

● ● ● ● ●

Meet Matthew. He has Down syndrome and is fully included in his classroom. In the past, he had a personal assistant who worked with him all day. She was responsible for helping with his self-care, eating, and instructional programs—just about everything. Matthew's educational team—classroom teacher, special educator, speech and language pathologist, personal assistant, and Matthew's mother—met weekly to plan and problem solve. As the years passed, Matthew's increasing dependence on his

Figure A

Words of Advice from the Principal

Context matters. What works in one school may not work in another, so approaches to change must always recognize the culture of the school and community, the beliefs and skill levels of individuals, and so forth.

Discussions about systems may be challenging, especially for people who view the current system as working well. Some people are comfortable stepping back and looking at the big picture; some prefer to talk at a concrete, action-oriented level; some are initially resistant to change. Forums for discussion must be varied and include large-group, small-group, and one-on-one discussions.

Leadership is critical and must recognize other leaders throughout the system. Change may be resisted if perceived as a top-down mandate. Challenges also exist in larger schools where multiple leaders may not agree with the premises of change. If such is the case, resistance within the leadership must be addressed before more change can occur.

Vision is important, but so is management. It's hard to change a system that is not functioning well or is in a crisis-response mode. Such a system may require shoring up before it can move forward.

Systemic change is a big undertaking, so you may need to start small. Particularly when resistance is likely, change may need to start not with leaders in positions of authority, but with individuals throughout the system who are willing to try something new. It may be helpful to emphasize the moral and ethical aspects of inclusion, the degree to which inclusion is part of existing laws and regulations, and the positive, research-based outcomes for students with and without disabilities (see Chapter 3).

Skilled professionals are essential to significantly change systems. Particularly important are special educators who believe in an inclusive model and are skilled in consultation, specific curriculum areas, instructional approaches, and Individualized Education Program (IEP) development. If your staff does not already include skilled professionals, you need to identify resources and to hire mentors or consultants who can help individual teachers further their professional development within the context of their jobs.

Skill development for paraprofessionals is also critical. Skill development must emphasize the paraprofessional's role in an inclusive approach.

New roles and responsibilities must be carefully defined and viewed for their potential to bring both intended and unintended consequences. We can learn from schools whose initial approach to inclusion was to hire more paraprofessionals to work with individual students in classrooms. Although that approach was intended to encourage inclusion, it allowed some classroom teachers to avoid taking full responsibility for meeting the needs of students who have wide-ranging skills and abilities.

assistant became clear. He did not seek his peers for assistance, his instructional programs were largely the responsibility of his assistant, and no one understood him as she did. The team knew that if the trend were to continue, Matthew would not become the independent learner that he needed to be. With the integrated service delivery approach that had taken shape on the porch, the classroom teacher, special educator, and speech and language pathologist now share responsibility for providing instruction on Matthew's individualized programs. The paraprofessional moves about the classroom and helps all students. Matthew's classmates are coached on how to reinforce Matthew's use of social skills. As a result of the shift in supports, Matthew has become a much more flexible and independent learner. The sight of Matthew walking home arm in arm with his classmates and friends is thrilling.

These two examples illustrate the changes that have occurred at Cook Hill Elementary School. First, as educators carried out their new, integrated vision of inclusion, people began to work collaboratively and to pick up new skills from their partners. The speech and language pathologists (SLPs), who had previously used a clinical model, now provided instruction within the context of the literacy curriculum. Classroom teachers picked up skills in differentiated instruction, curriculum adaptations, and classroom management from the team of special educators. Support personnel (e.g., special educators and SLPs) refined expertise in areas such as mathematics assessment and interventions for children with autism so they could better design individual student programs and enhance the general knowledge of their teams.

Second, the supports became more "melded." For instance, remedial reading instructors and literacy assistants worked together with special education teachers to coordinate their resources and reduce the number of specialists that any classroom teacher had to work with, and vice versa.

Third, the roles of the paraprofessionals and special educators transformed. Before the porch conversations, the school had 12 instructional assistants supervised by one special educator. They worked almost exclusively with those students who had the greatest needs. They became increasingly responsible for making key decisions and providing instruction for those students. The assistants had adequate training and materials, but there were concerns about the inclusiveness of this specialized role.

Fast forward to the present. Six, rather than twelve, paraprofessionals are assigned to classrooms to assist in differentiating curriculum and instruction rather than working with specific students. Two additional special educators were hired to replace the six eliminated and to provide direct, in-class support to all students. Brief out-of-class diagnostic sessions occur only if needed.

Three special educators increase the human resources for training and supervising paraprofessionals. Further, by combining school-based literacy funding with special education funding to pay salaries, paraprofessionals are now legitimately paid to assist all students (not just those eligible for special education) who may not meet the standards.

Sustaining Change Through New Structures and Professional Development

Our multidisciplinary group meets regularly. What should we call ourselves? Support services? We're not just that. How about "Skilled Others"? That's how we eventually came to be known as the S.O.s (or the "so and so's"). We are educators without classrooms. We are special educators, speech and language pathologists, remedial reading teachers, guidance counselors, school psychologists, administrators, and others who may join. Previously, we worked in isolation with our caseloads, seeing each other only occasionally at evaluation planning and IEP meetings. We'd pick each other's brains about particular issues as we passed in the hallway or we'd talk late after school when most others had left. We wanted more regular time together to collaborate around individual learners and the support systems in our school. Thus we formed the S.O. team. We now meet weekly to celebrate and collaborate. This weekly think tank is a powerful way to keep our system of support services vital and responsive.

*We challenge each other. We support each other. We solve prob-
lems together. Ideas flow among classroom teachers, individual
student teams, and the S.O. team.*

The S.O. is an example of several new team structures that evolved
to support the work of our inclusive school. Other critical teams
included (1) a teacher leadership team, the Faculty Advisory; (2)
three House Teams that brought together classroom teachers, special educators, and other support staff members weekly to discuss
common concerns; (3) a multidisciplinary prereferral team, the Educational Support Team, which developed plans for students who
struggled in school but were not eligible for special education; and
(4) ad hoc, cross-grade Vertical Teams comprising teachers, administrators, and paraprofessionals and formed, as needed, to address
specific topics (e.g., school climate, curriculum development).

Several factors influenced the success of the various teams.
The school schedule was carefully structured to allow specific meeting times for each team. Team members commit to attend regularly—a schoolwide norm. Each team gathers and summarizes
progress data, then regularly shares that data with the Faculty Advisory. Using the data, the Advisory team assesses and identifies gaps
in the education system and takes needed steps toward improvement. The House Teams ensure comprehensive and diverse adult
expertise. For example, each team would have a specialist (e.g., Title
I or reading teacher) with expertise in literacy and a specialist (e.g.,
special educator) with expertise in behavior management, collaboration, and curriculum and instruction differentiation to complement
the curriculum expertise of grade-level classroom teachers.

Cook Hill, like any system, found that individuals and teams
need ongoing skill development and incentives to sustain their work
and to retool. Professional development opportunities are formally
arranged for faculty and staff members, with some topics revisited
regularly. A recent example involved schoolwide workshops and
technical support on collaboration and teaming (Thousand & Villa,
2000), including skills such as using meeting minutes, roles, group
norms, and follow-up procedures.

The future of Cook Hill Elementary School rests in a culture of professionalism that invites ongoing conversation and reflection on ways to best educate a diverse student body. Teachers, paraprofessionals, and administrators have found that they learn as much by talking with one another and asking for help as they do by attending workshops and courses. One teacher commented, "Once you have the desire to learn more, everything else falls into place. A lot of learning is by example." Ongoing capacity building has resulted in the development of positive relationships, an increased sense of competence and responsibility among teachers and staff, and, ultimately, a new generation of inclusion and better outcomes for all students.

The *Circle of Courage* philosophy has become a common language and a framework for decision making at Cook Hill. It has helped educators expand their view of what is important in education to include the social and emotional development of children and to understand that *all* children are our responsibility.

References

Brendtro, L. K., Brokenleg, M., & Van Bockern, S. (1997). *Reclaiming youth at risk: Our hope for the future* (2nd ed.). Bloomington, IN: National Educational Service.

Thousand, J. S., & Villa, R. A. (2000). Collaborative teaming: A powerful tool in restructuring. In R. A. Villa & J. S. Thousand (Eds.), *Restructuring for caring and effective education: Piecing the puzzle together* (2nd ed., pp. 254–292). Baltimore: Paul H. Brookes.

Keepers of the Dream

Deborah Tweit-Hull

Kelvin entered O'Farrell Community School in the 7th grade. He had recently been released from a 24-hour residential facility for students with emotional disabilities. Because O'Farrell had no special education classes, Kelvin went from an extremely restrictive residential setting to a general education setting overnight. Mr. Evans, the special education teacher who supported Kelvin and the other students eligible for special education in Educational Family VI (the school is organized into six families that function as smaller schools within the school) described Kelvin as "a highly intelligent yet troubled child with a short fuse." When the school year started, Kelvin was involved in daily altercations (usually fights) with other students. If he wasn't fighting, he usually had a hand in orchestrating the resulting turmoil!

This story could have ended with Kelvin returning to the residential facility—or worse. However, Kelvin was in a school that had a dream, and he was included in that dream. The dream was that all students can succeed and be contributing members of the school and society. Mr. Evans and Kelvin's general education teachers were determined to make that happen. Being at O'Farrell exposed Kelvin to positive role models, taught him to get along with classmates and neighbors, and helped him believe in his teachers' high expectations for his behavior and academics.

By the end of his 8th grade year, Kelvin had raised his grades from a beginning level (1s on a 4-point rubric) to the

*developing and accomplished levels (2s and 3s). He rarely
missed class because of behavioral issues and graduated from
middle school with an earned scholarship that he could apply
toward college tuition. Had Kelvin gone to any other middle
school or junior high, he most assuredly would have been placed
in a special class for students with emotional disabilities and then
returned to a residential facility, never having a chance to
achieve the O'Farrell dream. Fortunately for Kelvin and our society, that nightmare did not happen.*

The O'Farrell School Dream

O'Farrell Community School was "born" in 1990 after a year and a
half of planning by teachers, administrators, and community members. The original Dream Team's vision for the school is reflected in
this mission statement:

> The O'Farrell Community School: Center for Advanced Aca-
> demic Studies will promote excellence by providing all middle-
> level students a single, academically enriched curriculum
> within a multiethnic, student-centered environment. The mis-
> sion of the school is to attend to the social, intellectual, psy-
> chological, and physical needs of middle-level youth so they
> will become responsible, literate, thinking, and contributing
> citizens.

The Dream Team also developed a set of values, the first of which
states, "All students can succeed academically, given the opportunity to learn through active participation." Fortunately for Kelvin,
"all" does mean *all* at O'Farrell.

As an urban charter school in California, O'Farrell educates
more than 1,500 middle-level students in grades 6 to 8. The diverse
students are Filipino, African American, Hispanic, Indochinese (primarily Lao), and Anglo American. Of the 1,500 students, 165 have
identified special education needs. The school has been a member of
the Coalition for Essential Schools since 1991. It uses the 10

principles established by the coalition to guide decisions and to evaluate practices and outcomes (see http://www.essentialschools.org
for more information).

The school is governed by the Community Council, which is
made up of a majority of teachers (50 percent plus one), with remaining members being students, parents, community members, support staff members, and the chief educational officer (CEO).
O'Farrell's CEO is the primary administrator. Other administrative
positions have largely been converted into teacher positions, thus
enabling O'Farrell to have the smallest class sizes of any secondary
school in the district. Although the school is large by most standards, it is organized into six Educational Families, thus creating a
feeling of community and belonging for staff members, students, and
parents. Each Educational Family serves approximately 260 students in the 6th, 7th, and 8th grades who are taught by an interdisciplinary team of teachers (i.e., humanities [English and social
studies], mathematics, science, the arts and music, physical education, and technology).

Addressing a Dream/Reality Mismatch

Although the intention of the founding Dream Team was to create a
school in which all students were educated together regardless of
label, the first five years saw a gradual separation of students with
more significant disabilities, specifically students labeled as having
severe or emotional disabilities. The separation was clearly incon-
sistent with the charter school's vision. The special education delivery model was also incompatible with the Educational Family
structure of the school, because special educators were serving students by category rather than by Educational Family, thus spreading
student support across several Families and teachers. The problem
was compounded by each Educational Family having a unique
schedule and way of doing business that made scheduling across
Families a nightmare. A group of teachers, including the special education team, needed to eliminate this mismatch of inclusive vision
and exclusionary reality.

The vision, skill building, incentives, resources, and action planning model of complex change, described in detail in Chapter 4, is a framework that worked well to describe the outcomes of this new talk about change that occurred as a result of this group's work.

Re-Visioning

From its beginning as a charter school, O'Farrell had a clearly articulated vision. However, it needed to re-examine its mission, or vision, for at least two reasons. The first was the vision to reality mismatch. Second, the impending charter renewal prompted discussions of whether inclusion would remain a central theme of the charter and the school. The special education group voiced issues about the charter mission and found support from the CEO, other teachers, and staff members. Having secured additional support from a local university that promoted inclusion in local schools, the Community Council gave a "green light" to plan for including all students. It took more than a year of tinkering and trials to develop a cross-categorical service delivery model to support students in Educational Families. Each Educational Family included a heterogeneous group of students eligible for special education. Consistent with the heterogeneous model already in place, students with disabilities were distributed across the six Families, and each of the school's special educators was assigned to support the teachers and students in one of those Families.

Building Skills

Skill building had been a priority throughout the school's charter years, but the focus now turned to building skills in differentiated instruction and team building. Special educators delivered workshops for faculty members on how to accommodate the educational needs of students with disabilities in the classroom. Special educators also concentrated on developing their own skills by attending conferences about inclusive education. A local business partner provided resources to conduct retreats for building teams. This training was a strategic move, because new special educators had been hired as a result of attrition and an increased number of students eligible for special education. Retreats have grown to include the larger school staff, and recent professional development topics have turned to schoolwide efforts to differentiate instruction and to establish specific programs that increase the literacy skills of all students. Support from grant-funded projects has also allowed for intensified training, support, and collaboration with paraprofessionals, whose experience and research have been central to successful inclusive education efforts.

Incentives

Some of the incentives for remaining and becoming better at being an inclusive school are intrinsic: being part of a supportive team, seeing students succeed, and being part of something innovative and exciting. More external incentives have included support to attend conferences and workshops and occasional extra pay for "going the extra mile" outside of school hours (not taking time from student support during regular school hours).

Resources

The cross-categorical model to deliver services has been a tremendous resource to everyone in the school. The special educators, now referred to as education specialists, have found their work much easier now that they have one Family rather than several Families of teachers and students to support. Classroom teachers who have worked at other schools comment that never have they experienced such a supportive environment and helpful special education staff. Having a common preparatory period and shared space also facilitated collaboration within the Family.

The education specialists and other support staff members have created their own support group to share information and materials and to create time for solving problems together. This group, known as the Home Base, meets three times a week for half an hour during the early morning. The group agreed to three rather than one or two meetings per week because members believe they can proactively address issues that arise throughout the week and engage in frequent face-to-face team building, sharing, and support in that amount of time. Early morning meetings do not interfere with common preparation time that the education specialists spend with their respective Educational Families during the physical education period five days a week.

The new schoolwide learning center, created from an old band room, provides space and physical opportunity to more readily collaborate. Half of the large space contains cubicles for each of the education specialists, who take advantage of their proximity to collaborate informally. In the other half, the learning center becomes a resource for all teachers and students and is equipped with computers, worktables, and supplemental materials and programs for students. There is also space for a secretary-clerk, a common resource library, and three smaller rooms with doors off the main room that can be used for testing as well as family and other confidential meetings. Finally, the 19 paraprofessionals, who are invaluable front-line primary resources to all teachers and students, have their own space in this larger room.

The O'Farrell Community Council has chosen to support the special education staff with a full-time secretary-clerk. The position has been invaluable, given all the paperwork and scheduling-related tasks required of special educators. The clerk schedules itinerant staff, outside assessments, and meetings of all sorts; makes copies; helps maintain student files; and performs other time-consuming tasks so education specialists and paraprofessionals can spend more time in the classrooms with students.

Another added human resource is a lead teacher among the special education staff. This resource proved necessary because O'Farrell has no assistant principals or administrators other than the CEO. Although the education specialists work under the direction of the teacher leader of their respective Educational Families, they found they needed a "departmental" lead teacher—who has a reduced (half) caseload—to manage the many special education administrative tasks. The lead teacher has enabled the other education specialists to spend more time with students in class.

Appointing a lead teacher rose out of necessity, opportunity, and creative thinking in restructuring resources. Because of increasing numbers of students with special needs, the special education staff grew from six to eight. Each of the six Educational Families kept one education specialist. The extra positions have been used to create the half-time position and to provide needed support in the 6th grade.

Action Planning

Action planning has always been a major part of the "O'Farrell way." One O'Farrell teacher said, "This school collects lots of data that we examine on a regular basis. Data provide the basis for a lot of the decision making that goes on at the school." At the end of each school year, all school departments must provide a comprehensive report to the Community Council describing activities, personnel, costs, and outcomes. The reports provide accountability, facilitate the Community Council's understanding of the effect of the initiatives that it has funded, and help guide decision making in planning future action to improve student performance and school climate.

The school has also secured external funding to conduct annual in-depth surveys of parent satisfaction. The survey results are used to determine ways to better connect with and support students and their families. Finally, the education specialists go beyond the legally required six-week report card progress reporting procedure and provide each student with a comprehensive written report describing progress toward individualized educational goals and overall progress within each class. In summary, a great deal of data are generated and used to plan future action regarding students, programs, and schoolwide initiatives.

Lessons from Keeping the Dream

The O'Farrell School has been open for more than a decade, and its evolution toward true inclusion has taught its teachers some important lessons about change, including the following:

- *Leadership counts!* Administrators who actually lead (not simply support from the rear) set the tone. Leadership among teachers is necessary, and a formal teacher leader within the department is invaluable, especially when embarking on new territory and supporting new teachers.

- *Together we're better—that is, collaboration counts!* Meaningful things can happen with time, shared space, and people willing to collaborate.
- *Community and a sense of belonging count!* Everyone (staff and students) is valued and makes contributions: parents and families, paraprofessionals, other support staff members, teachers, students, and administrators.
- *Professional and personal development count!* Teachers at O'Farrell see themselves as learners in this process. Last year's staff development activities centered around differentiated instruction. Staff members take the time and make the effort to attend conferences and trainings—with or without monetary support.
- *A little extra help counts!* Human resources, especially clerical support, prove invaluable to increasing contact with students or increasing collaboration with a "critical friend," which might lead to occasional monetary resources to support the work.
- *Kids count!* Ultimately, staff members at O'Farrell work hard to put students first. They have a dream and put in the time and effort required by their expanded roles and job descriptions so they can make dreams come true.
- *Count on this: change is a process, and we never stop growing and evolving!* Restructuring, reform, and inclusive schooling are not outcomes; they are an ongoing process to ensure that best practice always occurs.

O'Farrell has seen many teachers and staff members come and go. The school has grown, dealt with the budget implications of escalating energy costs, and felt the pressures of high-stakes assessments. Yet the values and the mission remain true to the original dream, as do the staff members, students, and parents who are the true keepers of the dream.

Chapter 5

Similar to your critique # of article

Promising Practices That Foster Inclusive Education

Alice Udvari-Solner, Jacqueline S. Thousand, Richard A. Villa,
Alice Quiocho, and M. G. (Peggy) Kelly

The inclusive education movement has often been viewed as a separate initiative running parallel or even counter to other curricular and instructional reform efforts. We take a more holistic, rather than separatist, view and propose that innovative changes to promote student success in general education are the same changes required for effective inclusion.

Many established and emerging general education practices emulate the principles of inclusive education (Cole, 2001). When these practices are used, educators are better equipped to facilitate meaningful and effective inclusive education not only for students perceived as disabled, at risk, or gifted, but also for the "allegedly average" students. Among the initiatives that have great promise for building inclusive schools are (1) universal design (Rose & Meyer, 2002), (2) differentiated instruction (Tomlinson, 1999, 2001), and (3) multiple intelligence theory (Armstrong, 2000). Chapter 6 examines how these three initiatives can be used to promote inclusive education. Additional best practice initiatives include 13 that this chapter examines in light of inclusive education:

- Constructivist learning theory
- Culturally relevant and responsive pedagogy
- Balanced approach to literacy instruction
- Interdisciplinary curriculum
- Authentic assessment of student performance

- Multiage grouping
- Use of looping
- Extended block scheduling
✓ • Use of technology in the classroom
- Multiple instructional agents in the classroom
✓ • Peer-mediated instructional approaches
✓ • Responsibility and peacemaking taught in the curriculum
- Creation of community schools

Constructivist Learning Theory

Constructivism is a theory of learning based on the historical works of Dewey, Piaget, and Vygotsky (Foote, Vermette, & Battaglia, 2001). From the perspective of constructivism, learning is the creation of meaning that occurs when an individual makes connections, associations, and linkages between new knowledge and existing knowledge (Grennon Brooks, 2002; Poplin & Stone, 1992). Accordingly, learners are described as "constructing" their own knowledge (Peterson, Fennema, & Carpenter, 1988–89) as they encounter new information and experiences that challenge their current understandings. To foster a child's power in the process of construction, meaningful learning occurs within an authentic situation and with authentic tasks.

Constructivism questions the assumptions and practices of reductionism that have pervaded our educational practices for generations. It recognizes learning as a complex process that defies linear prescriptions (Grennon Brooks & Brooks, 1999; Peterson & Knapp, 1993). In reductionism, effective learning takes place only in a rigid, hierarchical progression. Curriculum is often dissected and ordered into unrelated parts. The underlying premise is that children are unable to learn higher-order skills unless they master lower-order skills first (Peterson, Fennema, & Carpenter, 1988–89).

In contrast, these characteristics and practices exist in constructivist classrooms: (1) big curricular concepts are pursued and presented from whole to part, (2) students are encouraged to question concepts and explain their reasoning as an essential part of learning, (3) social discourse among students is valued and necessary to understand and transform each other's learnings, and (4) teachers and students jointly examine enduring concepts (Grennon Brooks & Brooks, 1999).

Conceptualizing curriculum and instruction from a constructivist view intersects productively with practices of inclusive education. Constructivism fosters the ideas that all people are always learning, the process is ongoing, and the interaction among students with varying abilities promotes conceptual growth. Constructivist thinking implies that learning is idiosyncratic and needs few, if any, prerequisites to build meaning. Teachers try to meet students at their current level of understanding and then help them connect and expand conceptions, without focusing on remediation. Inherent in this theoretical approach is the belief that all students enter school with different knowledge that is influenced by background, experiences, and cultural practice. Consequently, teachers must take those factors into account and ensure that new information is meaningfully related to the learner's existing knowledge.

Culturally Relevant and Responsive Pedagogy

Our nation's schools are increasingly diverse, with students from multicultural backgrounds equaling or, in urban areas, outnumbering students with European American roots. The rise in racially and ethnically diverse students has not been met with a corresponding supply of diverse teachers (Gordon, 2000). The situation often leaves students and teachers in a state of cultural incongruence in which expectations and values of the home and school environments differ vastly (Gay, 2000). The disproportionate numbers of culturally diverse students referred to special education has in part been attributed to this disjuncture between the teacher's standard pedagogy and the learning needs of students who are part of this changing demographic (Losen & Orfield, 2002).

In light of that burgeoning dilemma, Ladson-Billings (1995b) called for a more coherent and conscious link between schooling and culture. In her work with exemplary teachers of African

American students, she defined the theory and practice of culturally relevant pedagogy. Three major principles underpin that practice:

1. Teachers use students' culture to promote their academic achievement. By investigating and promoting what issues students find meaningful, teachers empower their learners to choose academic excellence (Ladson-Billings, 1995a).
2. Students must maintain or develop their own cultural competence. Teachers communicate that a student's cultural identity does not need to be compromised to succeed in the classroom. The unique aspects of a student's dress, language, and cultural experiences are welcomed and used in the classroom as vehicles for learning.
3. Students must see themselves as citizens who critically challenge cultural norms and the resulting social inequities. Teachers assist students to see their political positions in the community and world (Lipman, 1995).

These principles acknowledge that culture is a significant factor that affects teaching and learning (Webb-Johnson, 2002). Teachers who uphold the dynamics of culturally relevant pedagogy are practicing inclusive education as they impart influential messages that each child brings value to the classroom and that each child is powerful in directing his or her own achievement.

Balanced Approach to Literacy Instruction

Being literate is more than being able to automatically decode the words on a page. It is more than retelling a story or answering questions that assess comprehension. It includes, yet surpasses, the ability to predict, hypothesize, summarize, write fluently, and critique and generate questions about text. Being literate is complex. It means a person can determine what to do to make meaning of various sources— books, newspapers, magazines, journals, computer screens, the visual arts, mathematics, the sciences, and all types of media encountered in society, including signs, speeches, and music. It means being open to the perspectives of others.

Becoming literate is also complex. It requires time and supportive contexts in which reading, writing, and talking about reading and writing occur each day. It requires reading from many materials, including those of interest and personal choice. It also requires instruction that points out the relevance between what one reads or writes and what one's personal life and culture are. Most important, educators must acknowledge that becoming literate happens differently for each individual. Therefore, no single program, strategy, or approach will necessarily be effective with all students (Darling-Hammond, French, & Garcia-Lopez, 2002).

Given the complexities of being and becoming literate, a balanced approach to literacy instruction is currently advocated for a school to be truly inclusive (Tompkins, 1998). A balanced approach means that attention is paid to all processes that students use to make meaning of their lives. Specifically, a balanced approach must include the following:

- Literature that exposes students to world experiences.
- Oral language development that encourages students to question the world around them, as well as their own thoughts.
- A focus on developing students' language system (e.g., phonemic awareness, phonics, syntactical structures, grammar, language conventions such as capitalization and punctuation) to support their understanding of how language works and how they use language to get things done.
- Decodable and predictable text that scaffolds students' efforts to read independently.
- A strong emphasis on comprehension and critical thinking that prompts students to continuously question the texts, sources, and ideas that they encounter.
- Writing that provides an opportunity for students to share their thinking and voices with others.

Although the previous paragraph suggests specific literacy instructional strategies, we must remember that any strategy must evolve from data collected about and with students. At a minimum, teachers must take the time to do the following:

- Determine students' interest.
- Learn about students' backgrounds.
- Find ways to activate students' background knowledge.
- Take time to observe students while they are working.
- Assess and build students' background knowledge if content is unfamiliar.
- Analyze students' work over time to determine strengths and weaknesses.
- Connect instruction to curriculum standards, given the above data.

If my teacher only knew that I have never ever seen someone like me in the stories I read. If she did, she might take the time to select novels where I can read about people like me. I might like reading and school a lot better. (V. Audato, personal communication, spring 1997)

This reply was from a high school student who was asked what he wished his teachers knew about him. He states the importance of students seeing themselves in the literature and textbooks that they read. It is important that students read about a variety of cultures, that students of color and students with disabilities see themselves in the media used in all content areas, and that students read authentic literature written by authors who represent their cultures. To promote equitable, empowering, and balanced literacy development, educators must research and find materials that not only address curriculum standards and represent class members' cultural backgrounds, but also portray the protagonists as models rather than as victims of oppression. They must capture students' interests through genre types and reading topics (Jimenez, 2001; Nieto, 1999; Perez & Torres-Guzman, 2002).

Interdisciplinary Curriculum

> Curriculum integration is a curriculum design that is concerned with enhancing the possibilities for personal and social integration through the organization of curriculum around significant problems and issues, collaboratively identified by educators and young people, without regard for subject-area boundaries. (Beane, 1997, pp. x–xi)

An interdisciplinary approach can be considered a curricular orientation that expressly uses methodology and language from more than one discipline to examine a central theme, issue, problem, topic, or experience (Ellis & Stuen, 1998; Jacobs 1989; Wineburg & Grossman, 2000). Teachers and students are encouraged to examine one area in depth from multiple perspectives. Themes selected for instructional attention are big ideas that have relevance in the lives of the students to whom they will be taught (Ellis & Stuen, 1998). The nature of interdisciplinary approaches transcends the goal of gaining basic knowledge as it engages adults and students in group processes involving higher-level thinking and communication skills (Pate, Homestead, & McGinnis, 1997; Post, Ellis, Humphreys, & Buggey, 1997).

Interdisciplinary curriculum may be implemented through many methodologies and is well established at the elementary level. Individual teachers commonly interface the content of assorted disciplines throughout one unit of study. Classroom teachers may also join with instructors of art, music, and physical education to infuse the central theme across the student's instructional day.

Most true to the interdisciplinary philosophy is the practice at the middle school and high school levels of uniting teachers of separate disciplines in team teaching around a selected set of issues. Movement toward an interdisciplinary curriculum approach at the secondary level promotes an alternative to the balkanization that commonly exists when departments function in isolation and teachers rarely, if ever, interact or collaborate with those who teach different subjects (Hargreaves, 1994). The opportunity to jointly plan interdisciplinary curricula has the power to break down the privatization that permeates so many school cultures. Efforts to construct interdisciplinary approaches at the secondary level have also prompted a re-examination of traditional schedules and time blocks for instruction that have traditionally kept teachers apart. Resistance remains at the secondary level, however, in part because of the deep institutional structures that support discipline-based teaching, plus the real pressure that subject-based teachers feel to cover substantial amounts of material in a given year. Proposals toward curriculum integration are often perceived as compromising the integrity of a discipline and risking surface-level treatment of a subject (Wineburg & Grossman, 2000).

Interdisciplinary approaches have grown out of dissatisfaction with discipline-based or subject-driven methods of curriculum organization. Discipline-based models are premised on the teaching of content knowledge, but knowledge in all areas of study is growing exponentially each day. Essentially, there are not enough hours each day to teach it all within a school curriculum. Consequently, teachers need to prioritize what should be taught and what could be eliminated. Advocates of an interdisciplinary curriculum believe that learning can be structured to combat the narrow specialization that has accompanied the knowledge explosion of the computer age by designing curricula to help students see patterns across the chaos of diverse content (Wineburg & Grossman, 2000). Fragmentation of schedules and subject matter into allotted periods is common practice in discipline-based approaches. Students using curriculum integration methods are not forced to create bridges from seemingly unrelated splinters of information; instead, they view issues in a holistic manner. Indeed, some discipline-related skills may be intuitively taught in discrete ways. However, an interdisciplinary orientation should prompt teachers to search for sensible connections between disciplines that can contribute effectively to a deeper understanding of a concept or theme.

If discipline-based approaches pose such drawbacks for the typical population, the effect on students with disabilities is likely to be more significant. Students with disabilities have met with failure in general education classes primarily because the subject matter is unrelated, out of context, and practiced only a few minutes per day without consideration of generalization and transfer (Graham & Harris, 1999). Curriculum integration offers a method to show students how different subject areas influence their lives, thereby demonstrating the relevance of what is to be learned (Ackerman & Perkins, 1989; Beane, 1990, 1997).

Authentic Assessment of Student Performance

As schools shift to include differentiated, multicultural, constructivist, and interdisciplinary approaches, and as teachers place more emphasis on the meaning of learning with attention to children's interests and proclivities, better alignment between assessment and instruction becomes an obvious curricular need. Traditional measures of student performance rely primarily on recall of knowledge and provide decontextualized, snapshot views of students that are out of step with current dynamic, student-centered instructional practices—views unrelated to how students naturally use knowledge. For students with disabilities, the problem is amplified. When traditional, standardized, norm-referenced tests are used to measure student performance, the performance of students with disabilities falls predictably below that of their nondisabled peers, thus maintaining a deficit-oriented profile.

Out of a need for more realistic and responsive educational outcome measures, a number of alternative evaluation techniques referred to as "authentic assessments" have evolved. Authentic assessment occurs when students are expected to demonstrate skills that represent real-life learning demands in and out of the classroom, without contrived and standardized conditions (Lewin & Shoemaker, 1998; Tweit-Hull, Thousand, Bishop-Smith, & Falvey, 2000). Authentic assessments are learning exhibitions gathered over time to show a student's progress and applications. They involve observing students performing, producing, or demonstrating skills or responses in real-life contexts. For example, written expression may be assessed by using a portfolio that includes several samples of writing that represents conceptual ideas, rough drafts, self-edited papers, and final versions. The products may be poems, letters, or research papers that illustrate the ability to use other forms of written expression. The student is encouraged to self-evaluate and set personal goals for continued progress.

Authentic assessment strategies are important in creating inclusive classrooms in many ways. First, they provide valuable information about students' true abilities. Because authentic assessments allow teachers to observe students' discrepant or mastered skills, teachers are more likely to target instruction that is of the highest priority for individual students and the entire class. Thus, authentic assessments link overall classroom assessment with individualized, performance-based assessments that have been the preferred mode of assessment in special education. Second, authentic assessments are more likely to avoid cultural bias with students who are English-language learners and students who have cultural experiences different from those children upon whom traditional assessments are normed. Authentic assessment techniques allow for alternative views of intelligence (e.g., multiple intelligences theory, described in Chapter 6) and a longitudinal look at student progress over one or several years.

Multiage Grouping

Kasten & Lolli (1998) define multiage education as any deliberate grouping of children who are heterogeneous in age and grade to form a single classroom community that remains together for more than one academic year. Also referred to as nongraded, family, or vertical grouping, multiage classrooms are made up of a balanced collection of students with consideration for diversity in gender, learning strengths, ethnicity, interests, and age levels.

Multiage grouping—a practice well established by the 1990s in parts of the United States and in Canada, New Zealand, and Britain—is based on several underlying assumptions that directly oppose traditional grade-level grouping (Kasten & Clarke, 1993). Such grouping presumes that students of the same age have like learning needs and abilities and will benefit from similar instruction. Placement is based solely on age. Learning by grade level is viewed as a predictable, sequential, and orderly procedure yielding a "one year of schooling" product that can be judged and rated by a standard of performance. Additional drawbacks are that age-grading labels and limits children unnecessarily, restricts collaboration, inhibits social relationships other than with same-aged peers, and discards relationships between parents and teachers after one short year (Leeds & Marshak, 2002).

In contrast, a multiage approach views learning as a continuous and dynamic process. Student diversity is essential, and differing needs are understood. In an effective multiage classroom, children are encouraged to learn at different rates and levels. The child's growth is biological and psychological rather than merely physical. Thus, learning experiences are developmentally appropriate.

Multiage grouping is gaining attention in middle and high schools (George & Lounsbury, 2000; Petrie, Lindauer, Dotson, & Tountasakis, 2001). George and Lounsbury (2000) note that students in a traditional middle school may see eight different teachers a day and share classes with hundreds of students. A strong impetus for considering multiage grouping at the secondary level is the need for stable peer groups and for relationships with adults at a time of significant mental, social, moral, sexual, emotional, and physical changes. A move to multiage configurations can also create a sense of smaller learning communities within large schools where students are often not known well by even one adult.

Many elements of multiage grouping that make it a sound practice for students without disabilities are the same elements that make it advantageous for students with disabilities. The emphasis on heterogeneity requires classroom organization that can accommodate children with different maturity levels and different intellectual levels. In fact, the diversity impedes "teaching to the middle" and the use of lockstep instructional methods aimed at a whole class or a specific grade level (Leeds & Marshak, 2002).

A sense of community among teachers and students can promote long-term networks to support all students, including those with disabilities. Transitions from setting to setting and from teacher to teacher are associated with recoupment, generalization, and social adjustment difficulties for some students with disabilities. These passages are reduced in nongraded groupings, and teachers have time to get to know a particular student, thereby better ensuring personalized instruction. Information gained about the child in one year can be used to plan learning for the next year without the risk of losing that knowledge in a transition to a new teacher. Such personal and academic benefits for students are coupled with the perceptions of teachers that their longitudinal relationship will positively influence students and that together they will more successfully meet goals with enduring meaning (George & Lounsbury, 2000).

Use of Looping

Looping is an organizational practice in which a single graded class stays with the same teacher for two or more years. At the end of the looping cycle, the teacher begins the cycle again with a new class of students. Looping can be used at all grade levels but has more commonly been used at primary and middle school levels.

As an educational practice, looping has been around since 1913 and is often used in Japanese and German schools and within Waldorf schools in the United States (Simel, 1998). It is compatible with inclusive education. For students, benefits are similar to those described for multiage classrooms. Namely, students experience a long-term network of classmates who are more likely to be emotionally supportive and to have (1) in-depth relationships, (2) reduced apprehension at the start of a new school year because of fewer transitions, (3) increased continuity in learning and personalized instruction because of the teacher's deeper knowledge of each student, and (4) overall enhanced learning (Gaustad, 1998). Looping also benefits teachers by facilitating their use of instructional strategies that depend on in-depth student knowledge and cooperative group learning (Hanson, 1995). Looping allows teachers to work with parents and students for longer periods.

Extended Block Scheduling

Extended block scheduling is an educational practice in which at least part of the daily schedule is organized into blocks of time that exceed 60 minutes (Cawelti, 1994). Block scheduling has numerous advantages that also serve the goals of inclusive education, including more flexible and productive classroom environments and decreased class size. Block scheduling is more frequently used in middle and high schools but has equal benefit for elementary schools (Canady & Rettig, 2001).

Use of Technology in the Classroom

Technology is a catalyst for transforming schools by fostering excitement in learning for all children. As Kyle Peck and Denise Dorricott (1994) of the Institute for the Reinvention of Education observed:

> To see students so engaged in learning that they lose track of time, to see a level of excitement that causes students to come to school early and stay late, and to have time to develop strong relationships with students and to meet their individual needs, allows educators to fulfill age-old dreams. (p. 147)

What is technology? It is more than a computer and software packages, and it reinvents itself almost daily. Given the current and expanding access to technology inside the classroom, the climate is extremely conducive to naturally including students who have disabilities and who need technology to communicate, express their knowledge, control their environment, or access the curriculum.

In the past, technology has been in the possession of only a few experts, such as the computer lab teacher or those who designed or programmed augmentative communication systems for students with communication limitations. Today, all teachers are expected to use technology in their classrooms.

Technological tools of the student with disabilities that once seemed too complex, cumbersome, or expensive (e.g., massive computers bolted to a table, voice-synthesized speech) have become or are becoming portable, affordable, and standard as hardware and software. Technology that seemed unusual for a single student is now usual and fits well in a classroom. Never before have educators been able to capitalize on technological advances to readily educate students who have different learning styles and rates or who rely on technological support to learn, communicate, and control their world.

The comments of Dutton and Dutton (1990) on using technology to support the inclusion and learning of students with disabilities in school still hold true:

> Remember that technology is not a "cure" for a disability; rather it is a tool for everyone in society. Focus should not be placed on how the equipment itself will work, but efforts should be placed toward developing strategies, utilizing effective teaching practices, and working with the strengths of all students in the class. Technology can help remove barriers, but it is people, working together, who learn and succeed. (p. 182)

Accommodations using common technological tools that support inclusion include, but are not limited to, the following:

- Raising the font size and changing the color of text to simplify and highlight the visual image.
- Using KidPix (http://www.learningcompanyschool.com) for younger children to allow the screen-reading capability to reinforce the written word.
- Using Inspiration software (http://www.inspiration.com), a semantic mapping tool, so students can record their ideas using the "rapid fire" mode and can go back and think about how the ideas are related by connecting and dragging the text boxes. The software can translate the semantic map into an outline form.

- Searching the Internet for visualizations of complex concepts to use as part of a lesson (i.e., use of universal design principles).
- Using the WebQuest (http://webquest.sdsu.edu) inquiry model to design online experiences so students spend more time focusing on using information at analysis, synthesis, and evaluation levels rather than looking for information.
- Introducing a chat-style interface so students can interact through an avenue other than speech.
- Introducing online inquiry tools such as the Educator's Reference Desk (http://www.eduref.org) or The Gateway (http://www.thegateway.org) for teachers, parents, and students to find appropriate resources.
- Using the closed captioning feature of television to link the written word with the spoken word.

Multiple Instructional Agents in the Classroom

Schools that have been successful in responding to student diversity have redefined the role of educators and other support personnel as collaborative team members who jointly plan, instruct, and address the daily challenges of teaching in today's diverse classrooms (see Chapter 4). A classroom teacher with a collaborative support team can readily access assistance from specialists and related services personnel without referring students to special education. Having multiple instructional agents in the classroom increases the instructor-to-student ratio and immediacy in diagnosing and responding to student needs.

Multiple adults should provide classroom support only when necessary to avoid inflicting "disabling help" on students who neither need nor want adult support. Thus, a paraprofessional may be best for classroom support rather than as a "velcroed" personal assistant for one student. Related services personnel (such as physical and occupational therapists) enable students to interact with the curriculum rather than supplant curriculum access by removing a student with special needs from instructional activities with other students.

Exactly how collaborative teaching partnerships work will vary from one team to another. However, several collaborative teaching models have been successful and are available to guide partnerships (National Study on Inclusive Education, 1995; Villa, 2002; Villa, Thousand, & Nevin, 2004). The models include the following:

- *Consultant model.* Support personnel provide assistance to the general educator, enabling her or him to teach all students in the inclusive class.
- *Parallel teaching model.* Support personnel (e.g., special educator, Title I teacher, psychologist, speech and language therapist) and the classroom teacher rotate among different heterogeneous groups of students in different sections of the general education classroom.
- *Supportive teaching model.* The classroom teacher takes the lead role, and support personnel rotate among the students.
- *Complementary teaching model.* A support person does something to complement the instruction provided by the classroom teacher (e.g., models note taking on a transparency, paraphrases the teacher's statements).
- *Coteaching model.* Support personnel teach alongside the general education teacher, sharing responsibility for delivering content, guiding student learning, and managing classroom behavior.

Some of these models (e.g., coteaching, complementary teaching) require greater commitment to, comfort with, and skill in collaborative planning and "role release" (i.e., passing the usual instructional responsibilities to someone else). However, in our collaborative teaching research, we learned that such partners usually find at least one model with which to start. Teaching teams can and are advised to use all models as team members grow in mutual trust, knowledge of others' content and expertise, and skill in problem solving and conflict resolution.

Peer-Mediated Instructional Approaches

Until recently, missing from the collaborative teaming quotient were the students themselves. Thousand, Villa, and Nevin (2002) point out that educators have a responsibility to model collaboration by sharing their decision-making and instructional power with students whom they invite to collaborate (1) as members of planning teams who determine accommodations for themselves or classmates with and without disabilities; (2) as advocates for themselves and classmates during meetings and other major events that determine a student's future educational and postschool choices; (3) as social and logistical support to a classmate as a peer partner or as a member of a *Circle of Friends* (Falvey, Forest, Pearpoint, & Rosenberg, 2002); (4) as coaches; and (5) as members of school governance committees such as the school board.

Cooperative Group Learning

Johnson and Johnson (2002) point out three ways that students may interact during learning. They may compete to see who is the best, they may work individually toward their goals, or they may have a stake in others' success by working cooperatively. Although many U.S. students view schooling as a competitive enterprise, competitive learning interferes with building a community—a primary objective of inclusive education.

There is a dramatic difference between asking students to sit together and work in a group and carefully structuring groups of students to work in cooperative learning groups. A group of children chatting at a table as they do their own work is not a cooperative group because there is no sense of positive interdependence or mutual support. Common to the diverse approaches of cooperative learning are five conditions or attributes: (1) a joint task or learning activity suitable for group work, (2) small-group learning in teams of five or fewer members, (3) use of cooperative behaviors, (4) positive interdependence as team members encourage one another's learning, and (5) individual accountability and responsibility for participation and learning (Davidson, 2002).

A rich research base supports the use of cooperative learning models to enable successful learning in heterogeneous groups of students with varying abilities, interests, and backgrounds. Within inclusive education, cooperative learning makes great sense as an instructional strategy because it enables students "to learn and work in environments where their individual strengths are recognized and individual needs are addressed" (Sapon-Shevin, Ayres, & Duncan, 2002, p. 209). Cooperative learning transforms the classroom into a microcosm of the diverse society and work world students will enter. Within that context, students learn to appreciate differences and a society in which each person is valued.

Partner Learning

Partner learning or peer tutoring systems are not new. Children teach one another informally when they play games and engage in sports. Teachers in one-room schoolhouses relied heavily on students as instructors. Peer tutor systems can be same-age or cross-age and can be established within a single classroom, across classes, or across an entire school. Partner learning systems build relationships among students and offer a cost-effective way of enhancing learning time. Evidence of the social, instructional, and cost benefits of tutoring are abundant (see LaPlant & Zane, 2002; McMaster, Fuchs, & Fuchs, 2002; Thousand, Villa, & Nevin, 2002). Students receiving such instruction experience learning gains, interpersonal skill development, and heightened self-esteem. Good and Brophy (1997) suggest that the quality of instruction delivered by trained tutors may be superior to that of adults for at least three reasons: (1) children use more age-appropriate and meaningful language and examples, (2) peer tutors recently learned what they are to teach and are familiar with their tutees' potential frustrations, and (3) peer tutors are more direct than adults.

Tutors also experience benefits similar to those of their tutees: namely, interpersonal skills are developed and self-esteem may be enhanced. Tutors report they understand the concepts, procedures, and operations that they teach at a much deeper level than before teaching—probably because of the metacognitive activity they engaged in while preparing to teach.

Responsibility and Peacemaking Taught in the Curriculum

The children who are perceived as the most challenging to educate within the current school structure are those who demonstrate high rates of rule-violating behavior, who have acquired maladaptive ways of relating, and who are perceived as troubled or troubling. Adversity at home and in the community negatively affects an increasing number of children's ability and motivation to learn. The educator's job has broadened from providing effective instruction and personalized accommodations to addressing the stressors in children's lives by offering many school-based social supports. Teaching responsibility and providing instruction in peacemaking have risen to the top as curriculum priorities (Villa, Udis, & Thousand, 2002).

Teaching Responsibility

Educators have long recognized that for students to master a content area such as math or sciences, they need continuous and complex instruction throughout their elementary, middle, and high school years. When a child does not learn a concept or skill, we react with a "teaching response" and attempt to reteach the material with additional or different supports and accommodations. However, the content area of "responsibility" does not receive the same immediate treatment. The explicit teaching of patterns of behavior and habits representative of responsible behavior rarely occurs; instruction is relegated to reactive, add-on, quick-fix methods. Teaching responsibility is as demanding as teaching any other curriculum area; it requires careful thought and complex, ongoing instruction from the day a child enters the school.

For students to learn responsible values, attitudes, and behaviors, they must first perceive that somebody in school genuinely cares about them. Teachers, above all, must demonstrate caring and concern by validating students' efforts and achievements. They must teach responsibility directly by establishing a schoolwide discipline that promotes learning responsibility; instructing students in prosocial communication skills, anger management, and impulse

115

control techniques; and setting limits to ensure safety (Villa, Udis, & Thousand, 2002).

Responsibility-based discipline models (see, Curwin & Mendler, 2001; Glasser, 1998) acknowledge conflict as a natural part of life. They cast the educator in the role of facilitator of conflict resolution rather than the role of cop who enforces "if–then" consequences (e.g., three tardies equal a detention, 10 absences result in a failing grade). In a responsibility-based discipline model, the teacher's response to a rule-violating behavior is not prescribed but depends on all kinds of factors (e.g., time of day, frequency and intensity of the behavior, number of other people exhibiting the behavior) and may range from reminders, warnings, redirections, cues, and self-monitoring techniques to behavioral contracts and direct teaching of alternative behaviors. Critical to developing student responsibility is the recognition by teachers and other educational leaders that the teaching of responsibility should (1) be part of the curriculum and considered as important as any other curriculum domain; (2) be concerned with teaching young people how to get their needs met in ways acceptable to society; and (3) include modeling, coaching, and ongoing thought and reflection on the part of school personnel.

Students as Peacemakers

An increasing number of schools in the United States are incorporating the development of student responsibility into the school's culture and curriculum by turning conflict management back to the students and using students as peer mediators. Students who are trained to be mediators are available during school hours to conduct mediations at the request of students, teachers, or administrators. A small number of students may be selected and trained in the mediation process, or all students may receive training in conflict resolutions skills. Students who serve as mediators are sometimes called *peacemakers* or *conflict managers*.

Schrumpf and Jansen (2002) outlined a structured process for establishing a peer mediation program in which students and teachers engage in up to 12 hours of training in the basic skills of negotiation and mediation. Adults can provide ongoing support to student peacemakers through regular meetings in which issues are discussed and additional training is provided. Peer mediation must be made highly visible so students and teachers actually use the program as an alternative to adult intervention.

Peer mediation requests and peer mediation agreements can be analyzed to determine the nature, frequency, and outcomes of mediation requests. Emerging data suggest that peer mediation programs are successful in decreasing discipline referrals, fights, student suspensions, and vandalism while improving school attendance (Schrumpf & Jansen, 2002). Learning to resolve conflicts with peers is an empowering action that is consistent with the principles of inclusive education and that has the potential to go from peace between two people to peacemaking in a community and global context.

Creation of Community Schools

A national interest exists in reconsidering educational institutions as supporters of the welfare of community members beyond the traditional concept of "schooling." The idea of community schools has developed in response to the social and educational needs of community members of all ages. Structurally, the school building becomes a support center for a network of agencies that coalesce to address community needs and expand learning opportunities for a wider range of community members.

At the core of the community school philosophy is the idea that students' academic achievement has a social context and that education is not isolated from the rest of the child's life (Children's Aid Society, 2001). The fundamental reason to intersect services is to ensure that children enter the classroom physically, emotionally, and socially more able to learn. Consequently, interrelated goals of the community school movement create stronger alliances between families and schools, build healthier and more resilient neighborhoods, and foster enduring linkages with and among community resources (Harkavy & Blank, 2002).

No single model typifies community schools, and because schools are tailored to local needs, they are as varied as their locales and residents. Community schools typically orchestrate an array of programs. The following list features representative examples:

1. Family resource centers have access to on-site health and learning services, emergency assistance, legal aid, employment assistance, and referral to related service providers.
2. Remedial and enrichment activities for children are outside usual school hours and during the summer.
3. Recreation, athletic, and arts programs exist for adults and children.
4. Cross-generational programs have community seniors in honored positions as instructional partners.
5. Adult education has classes in areas such as literacy, computer technology, General Education Development (GED) test preparation, and vocational training classes.
6. Programs and counseling services interface with the school day to address mental health concerns, issues of parenting, and interpersonal relationships.

Planning and implementation of services require a collaborative team or council. Members will most often include a lead community agency, school representatives, staff of social service organizations, parents and other community members, funders, and student delegates (Parson, 1999). To oversee the day-to-day programs and partnerships, a leadership position is usually created and is typically referred to as the community education coordinator. A combination of funding sources from school or city budgets; contributions from businesses and private donors; and grants from corporations, foundations, and federal or state governments, as well as fees paid by program participants, provides sustained capital for community school models (Decker & Boo, 1996, 1998).

The concept of community schools reinforces the ideals of inclusive education by embracing a wider constituency of membership when defining schooling. The activities that bring families and community people together to shape a responsive learning environment acknowledge that students, particularly those at risk of failure or exclusion, require a seamless system of support.

● ● ● ● ●

The exemplary or promising practices in this chapter establish the infrastructure within which the principles of inclusive education can be realized. Collectively, the initiatives can create a unified philosophy and revolutionary standards of educational practice. If widespread progress is to occur in education, inclusive education must not be treated as an add-on to other more pressing initiatives; it must be the central discussion, and teachers must be the central participants in a scholarly discourse. The interface between inclusive education and other exemplary practices must become clearly and publicly self-evident (Peterson & Knapp, 1993).

References

Ackerman, D., & Perkins, D. N. (1989). Integrating thinking and learning skills across the curriculum. In H. H. Jacobs (Ed.), *Interdisciplinary curriculum: Design and implementation* (pp. 77–95). Alexandria, VA: Association for Super vision and Curriculum Development.

Armstrong, T. (2000). *Multiple intelligences in the classroom.* Alexandria, VA: Association for Super vision and Curriculum Development.

Beane, J. (1990). Rethinking the middle school curriculum. *Middle School Journal, 21*(5), 1–5.

Beane, J. (1997). *Curriculum integration: Designing the core of democratic education.* New York: Teachers College Press.

Canady, R. L., & Rettig, M. (2001, January). *Block scheduling: The key to quality learning time.* Alexandria, VA: National Association of Elementary School Principals.

Cawelti, G. (1994). *High school restructuring: A national study.* Arlington, VA: Educational Research Service.

Children's Aid Society. (2001). *Building a community school* (3rd ed.). New York: Author.

Cole, R. (2001). *More strategies for educating everybody's children.* Alexandria, VA: Association for Supervision and Curriculum Development.

Curwin, R. L., & Mendler, A. N. (2001). *Discipline with dignity.* Upper Saddle River, NJ: Merrill Education/Prentice Hall, for Association for Supervision and Curriculum Development.

Darling-Hammond, L., French, J., & Garcia-Lopez, S. P. (2002). *Learning to teach for social justice.* New York: Teachers College Press.

Davidson, N. (2002). Cooperative and collaborative learning: An integrative perspective. In J. S. Thousand, R. A. Villa, & A. I. Nevin (Eds.), *Creativity and collaborative learning: The practical guide to empowering students, teachers, and families* (2nd ed., pp. 181–196). Baltimore: Paul H. Brookes.

Decker, L. E., & Boo, M. R. (1996). *Community schools: Linking home, school, and community.* Fairfax, VA: National Community Education Association. Available: http://ericweb.tc.columbia.edu/community/community_schools.

Decker, L. E., & Boo, M. R. (1998). *Community schools: Serving children, families, and communities.* Fairfax, VA: National Community Education.

Dutton, D. H., & Dutton, D. L. (1990). Technology to support diverse needs in regular classes. In W. Stainback & S. Stainback (Eds.), *Support networks for inclusive schooling: Interdependent integrated education* (pp. 167–183). Baltimore: Paul H. Brookes.

Ellis, E., & Stuen, C. (1998). *The interdisciplinary curriculum.* Larchmont, NY: Eye on Education.

Falvey, M. A., Forest, M. S., Pearpoint, J., & Rosenberg, R. L. (2002). Building connections. In J. S. Thousand., R. A. Villa, & A. I. Nevin (Eds.), *Creativity and collaborative learning: The practical guide to empowering students, teachers, and families* (2nd ed., pp. 29–52). Baltimore: Paul H. Brookes.

Foote, C., Vermette, P., & Battaglia, C. (2001). *Constructivist strategies: Meeting standards and engaging adolescent minds.* Larchmont, NY: Eye on Education.

Gaustad, J. (1998, December). *Implementing looping.* Clearinghouse on Educational Policy and Management, College of Education, University of Oregon. (ERIC Digest, University of Oregon. No. 123, EDO, EA-98-7).

Gay, G. (2000). *Culturally responsive teaching: Theory, research, and practice.* New York: Teachers College Press.

George, P., & Lounsbury, J. (2000). *Making big schools small: Multiage grouping, looping, and schools-within-a-school.* Westerville, OH: National Middle School Association.

Glasser, W. (1998). *The quality school: Managing students without coercion* (3rd ed.). New York: Harper and Row.

Good, T. L., & Brophy, J. G. (1997). *Looking into classrooms* (7th ed.). New York: Harper and Row.

Gordon, J. (2000). *The color of teaching.* New York: Routledge/Falmer Press.

Graham, S., & Harris, K. (1999). *Teachers working together: Enhancing the performance of students with special needs.* Brookline, MA: College Park.

Grennon Brooks, J. (2002). *Schooling for life: Reclaiming the essence of learning.* Alexandria, VA: Association for Supervision and Curriculum Development.

Grennon Brooks, J., & Brooks, M. (1999). *In search of understanding: The case for constructivist classrooms.* Alexandria, VA: Association for Supervision and Curriculum Development.

Hanson, B. (1995). Getting to know you: Multiyear teaching. *Educational Leadership, 53*(3), 42–43.

Hargreaves, A. (1994). *Changing teachers: Changing times.* New York: Teachers College Press.

Harkavy, I., & Blank, M. (2002). Community schools: A vision of learning that goes beyond testing. *Education Week, 21*(31), 38, 52.

Jacobs, H. H. (1989). The growing need for interdisciplinary curriculum content. In H. H. Jacobs (Ed.), *Interdisciplinary curriculum: Design and implementation* (pp. 1–13). Alexandria, VA: Association for Supervision and Curriculum Development.

Jimenez, R. T. (2001). Strategic reading for language-related disabilities: The case of a bilingual Latina student. In M. Reyes & J. Halcon (Eds.), *The best for our children: Critical perspectives and literacy for Latino students* (pp. 153–167). New York: Teachers College Press.

Johnson, D., & Johnson, R. (2002). Ensuring diversity is positive. In J. S. Thousand, R. A. Villa, & A. I. Nevin (Eds.), *Creativity and collaborative learning: The practical guide to empowering students, teachers, and families* (2nd ed., pp. 197–208). Baltimore: Paul H. Brookes.

Kasten, W. C., & Clarke, B. (1993). *The multi-age classroom: A family of learners.* Katonah, NY: Richard C. Owen Publishers.

Kasten, W. C., & Lolli, E. (1998). *Implementing multi-age education: A practical guide.* Norwood, MA: Christopher-Gordon Publishers.

Ladson-Billings, G. (1995a). Toward a theory of culturally relevant pedagogy. *American Educational Research Journal, 32*(3), 465–491.

Ladson-Billings, G. (1995b). But that's just good teaching: The case for culturally relevant pedagogy. *Theory into Practice, 34*(3), 159–165.

LaPlant, L., & Zane, N. (2002). *Partner learning systems.* In J. S. Thousand, R. A. Villa, & A. I. Nevin (Eds.), *Creativity and collaborative learning: The practical guide to empowering students, teachers, and families* (2nd ed., pp. 271–282). Baltimore: Paul H. Brookes.

Leeds, A., & Marshak, D. (2002). *Teaching and learning in the intermediate multi-age classroom.* Lanham, MD: Scarecrow Press.

Lewin, L., & Shoemaker, J. (1998). *Great performances: Classroom-based assessment tasks.* Alexandria, VA: Association for Supervision and Curriculum Development.

Lipman, P. (1995). "Bringing out the best in them": The contribution of culturally relevant teachers to educational reform. *Theory into Practice, 34*(3), 202–208.

Losen, D., & Orfield, G. (2002). *Racial inequity in special education.* Cambridge, MA: Harvard Education Press.

McMaster, K., Fuchs, D., & Fuchs, L. (2002). Using peer tutoring to prevent early reading failure. In J. S. Thousand, R. A. Villa, & A. I. Nevin (Eds.), *Creativity and collaborative learning: The practical guide to empowering students, teachers, and families* (2nd ed., pp. 235–246). Baltimore: Paul H. Brookes.

National Study on Inclusive Education. (1995). New York: City University of New York, National Center on Educational Restructuring and Inclusion.

Nieto, S. (1999). *The light in their eyes: Creating multicultural learning communities.* New York: Teachers College Press.

Parson, S. (1999). *Transforming schools into community learning centers.* Larchmont, NY: Eye on Education.

Pate, P. E., Homestead, E. R., & McGinnis, K. (1997). *Making integrated curriculum work: Teachers, students, and the quest for coherent curriculum.* New York: Teachers College Press.

Peck, K., & Dorricott, D. (1994). Why use technology? *Educational Leadership, 15*(7), 11–14.

Perez, B., & Torres-Guzman, M. (2002). *Learning in two worlds: An integrated Spanish/English biliteracy approach* (3rd ed.). Boston: Allyn and Bacon.

Peterson, P., Fennema, E., & Carpenter, T. (1988–89). Using knowledge of how students think about math. *Educational Leadership, 46*(4), 42–46.

Peterson, P., & Knapp, N. (1993). Inventing and reinventing ideas: Constructivist teaching and learning in mathematics. In G. Cawelti (Ed.), *Challenges and achievements of American education: 1993 yearbook of the Association for Supervision and Curriculum Development* (pp. 134–157). Alexandria, VA: Association for Supervision and Curriculum Development.

Petrie, G., Lindauer, K., Dotson, K., & Tountasakis, M. (2001). The nongraded middle school: Can it improve early adolescents? *Education, 121*(4), 781–786.

Poplin, M. S., & Stone, S. (1992). Paradigm shifts in instructional strategies: From reductionism to holistic/constructivism. In W. Stainback & S. Stainback (Eds.), *Controversial issues confronting special education: Divergent perspectives* (pp. 153–180). Boston: Allyn and Bacon.

Post, T., Ellis, A., Humphreys, A., & Buggey, L. A. (1997). *Interdisciplinary approaches to curriculum.* Upper Saddle River, NJ: Merrill Publishing.

Rose, D., & Meyer, A. (2002). *Teaching every student in the digital age: Universal design for learning.* Alexandria, VA: Association for Supervision and Curriculum Development.

Sapon-Shevin, M., Ayres, B., & Duncan, J. (2002). Cooperative learning and inclusion. In J. S. Thousand, R. A. Villa, & A. I. Nevin (Eds.), *Creativity and collaborative learning: The practical guide to empowering students, teachers, and families* (2nd ed., pp. 209–222). Baltimore: Paul H. Brookes.

Schrumpf, F., & Jansen G. G. (2002). The role of students in resolving conflict. In J. S. Thousand, R. A. Villa, & A. I. Nevin (Eds.), *Creativity and collaborative learning: The practical guide to empowering students, teachers, and families* (2nd ed., pp. 283–301). Baltimore: Paul H. Brookes.

Simel, D. (1998). Education for building: Teacher attitudes toward looping. *International Journal of Educational Reform, 7*(4), 330–337.

Thousand, J. S., Villa, R. A., & Nevin, A. I. (Eds.). (2002). *Creativity and collaborative learning: The practical guide to empowering students, teachers, and families* (2nd ed.). Baltimore: Paul H. Brookes.

Tomlinson, C. A. (1999). *The differentiated classroom: Responding to the needs of all learners.* Alexandria, VA: Association for Supervision and Curriculum Development.

Tomlinson, C. A. (2001). *How to differentiate instruction in mixed-ability classrooms* (2nd ed.). Alexandria, VA: Association for Supervision and Curriculum Development.

Tompkins, G. (1998). *50 literacy strategies.* Upper Saddle River, NJ: Merrill/Prentice Hall.

Tweit-Hull, D., Thousand, J. S., Bishop-Smith, K., & Falvey, M. (2000). Creating meaning through assessment for students with disabilities. In The Alliance for Curriculum Reform, *Assessing student learning: A practical guide* [CD ROM] (pp. 1–28). Cincinnati, OH: Author.

Villa, R. A. (2002). *Collaborative teaching: The co-teaching model* [Videotape]. Port Chester, NY: National Professional Resources.

Villa, R., Thousand, J., & Nevin, A. (2004). *A guide to co-teaching: Practical tips for facilitating student learning.* Thousand Oaks, CA: Corwin Press.

Villa, R. A., Udis, J., & Thousand, J. S. (2002). Supporting students with troubling behavior. In J. S. Thousand, R. A. Villa, & A. I. Nevin (Eds.), *Creativity and collaborative learning: The practical guide to empowering students, teachers and families* (2nd ed., pp. 135–156). Baltimore: Paul H. Brookes.

Webb-Johnson, G. (2002). Strategies for creating multi-cultural and pluralistic societies. In J. S. Thousand, R. A. Villa, & A. I. Nevin (Eds.), *Creativity and collaborative learning: The practical guide to empowering students, teachers, and families* (2nd ed., pp. 55–70). Baltimore: Paul H. Brookes.

Wineburg, S., & Grossman, P. (2000). *Interdisciplinary curriculum: Challenges to implementation.* New York: Teachers College Press.

Collaborative Teaching and Student Support: "Where Miracles Happen Every Day"

Nancy Frey, Douglas Fisher, and Denyse Patel Henry

Dwain glances around the 6th grade science classroom, unsure of what to do next. He is a member of a group of five students assigned to dissect a squid. Dwain has an Individualized Education Program (IEP), but the other members of his group do not. They've already located the creature's three hearts and the giant nerve that runs the length of its body. Juliette, another 6th grader, leans over to point to the next step on Dwain's lab sheet. "It says that we're supposed to remove the pen." Five heads lean in closely as Tran wields the scalpel to extract the thin strip of shell inside the squid's mantle. Triumphant, he displays the long, pointed, chitinous material and then dips it into the squid's ink sac. Looking around to make sure that no adult is lurking by too closely, Tran writes his name with the squid ink on a paper towel, then hands the slender shell to Dwain. Without a word passing between them, Dwain writes his name below Tran's, then looks up to share a conspiratorial grin with his lab partners.

A few tables away, the special educator working in this class smiles her own secret smile. She has witnessed this scene and is quite pleased. Sixth grade science is about learning the biology of cephalopods, but it is also about having a little surreptitious fun with your friends.

For schools, there is no singular path to inclusive practice. No two stories are the same, and the impetus for change is likely to be unique to each school. However, the outcomes seem to coalesce into a common theme: students with and without IEPs consistently make academic, social, and behavioral gains when inclusive practices occur (Fisher, Frey, & Thousand, 2003; McGregor & Vogelsberg, 1998). This "voice of inclusion" focuses on the three-year path of a school that opened each day with the affirmation, "Welcome to our school, where miracles happen every day."

Year 1—Convenient Inclusion

Palm Crest Intermediate School is in a large urban district in the southeastern United States (please note that all names are pseudonyms). The school was built to alleviate enrollment at an overcrowded elementary school nearby. However, construction delays slowed the opening, and Palm Crest found itself with an incomplete building and a shortage of space. Encouraged by members of the special education staff, the principal agreed to close a segregated special education classroom to free needed classroom space. By that singular act, inclusive education was poised to come to Palm Crest, as special education teachers and the students they served joined general education classrooms, teachers, and classmates.

The closing of the special education classroom was a "mainstreaming" rather than an inclusive educational move; that is, special educators traded on friendships and struck deals with general education teachers. For example, it was agreed that a paraprofessional or special education teacher would be in each classroom that had students with IEPs. Although that decision locked up resources, we saw it as a first step.

During the first year, a primary struggle was to get the vision of inclusion out there. A marriage of convenience necessitated by constraints of space began to yield observable and obvious academic and social progress for the first 20 students in general education classrooms. The positive change did not go unnoticed by teachers, students, and parents, who were uniformly pleased. Teachers were also pleased with the new professional partnerships. Building on that success in the second quarter of the school year, 20 students with cognitive disabilities who were still in a separate classroom joined the read-aloud time of two 5th grade classrooms, not because that was the grade in which they were enrolled, but because the teachers were willing to host the students.

What did we learn from this inclusion of convenience? We learned it works if students are on class rolls, are viewed as classmates, and are provided supports. We also learned that the 20 students who simply visited 5th grade classrooms remained just that—visitors. As the building took shape a mile away, we met frequently to take stock of these lessons and to plan how the following year might be different. We visited the principal, who approved our plan.

Year 2—Uneasy Inclusion

The second year brought not only a new building but also a reorganization of special educators' roles. A philosophical split still divided the special education personnel: two were opposed to working in general education classrooms, and two were eager to expand the practice. So we agreed to split duties according to ideology. Two of the special educators worked in general classrooms, and two remained in special education classrooms. The split didn't end there. We made another rookie mistake: namely, the two special educators working in general education served students according to labels. One supported students with learning disabilities while the other supported students with more significant disabilities in the same grades. Furthermore, the special educator who supported the students with more significant disabilities still spent the first two hours of each morning providing reading and mathematics instruction in a resource room. She quickly discovered that teaching in a resource room *and* supporting students in general education classrooms were two jobs rather than one.

What did we learn from our second year of "uneasy inclusion"? Variations of coteaching were fun and successful. In one 6th grade science classroom, coteachers fell into a pattern of standing across the room from one another, trading primary teaching responsibility every few minutes. Because students' attention volleyed back and forth between the two, we dubbed this style "ping pong teaching." In a 5th grade classroom, the teacher felt most comfortable leading instruction, so the special educator engaged in supportive teaching by jotting questions about the material on sticky notes and transferring them onto a K-W-L chart (Ogle, 1986). At the end of class, the notes were used to clarify understanding, summarize key points, and review concepts. The method proved useful for all the students in the class, not just those with IEPs for whom it was initially intended.

We learned that modifications and accommodations created for individual students became popular with the general education teachers, who saw how the changes reached other students. For example, when science teachers observed students failing their tests, they adopted tests initially designed for students with IEPs. One teacher remarked, "I can use these tests because the same big concepts are on it. It's not different from what I teach."

We learned that proximity combined with high expectations can lead to friendship. For the first time, we heard reports from parents that their children were being invited to outside social events by classmates. The opening vignette with Dwain took place during the second year at Palm Crest.

We learned from our mistakes, and we learned that rigid scheduling of adults creates problems. For example, because one special education support teacher also ran a resource room each morning for two hours, she was not available to handle any crises that occurred during that time. The situation frustrated general educators. We also learned that we were unprepared to change our coteaching structure to accommodate student growth. In the beginning, students with IEPs needed to learn how to take notes, work in groups, hand in assignments, and ask for help in ways that were consistent with the grade-level expectations. During the fall, much in-class support focused on those areas. But as spring arrived and students were comfortable with expectations, they needed less support. Unprepared to monitor and adjust our roles flexibly, we remained stuck in our schedule.

We learned a final lesson: as special educators, we needed to modify our own behavior in general education classrooms. Foolishly, we initially worked only with students with IEPs and passed by others who needed assistance. Students noticed and quickly identified who had an IEP and who did not. We remedied that shortcoming by instituting a "touch two, then you" pattern of giving assistance, stopping at the desks of two students without IEPs before reaching a student with the IEP. Our intention was to blur the lines in the classroom, but we found that in the process, our teaching and understanding of the curriculum improved.

Despite drawbacks of the service delivery plan that year, the good news spread and other teachers asked for our in-class support. We were most encouraged by some teachers publicly asking, "Couldn't every student be enrolled in a general education classroom?" We revised our service plan and visited the principal with yet another new proposal.

Year 3—Comprehensive Inclusion

Year 3 witnessed the closing of all special education classrooms and the creation of a learning lab (staffed by special educators on a rotating schedule) that was available to *all* students in the school. Each special educator provided in-class support to a particular grade rather than a category of students, and special education paraprofessionals were assigned to teachers rather than individual students.

A flexible and responsive continuum of adult and peer personal supports was made to provide students with the least intrusive and "only as necessary" support (Fisher, Frey, & Sax, 2004).

Adult and Peer Support Options

Support options available to students and teachers encompass four types of adult support (full-time adult support, scheduled adult support, intermittent adult support, and supplemental adult support) and two types of peer support (structured peer support and natural peer support).

Full-Time Adult Support. Some students require adult proximity for the duration of the class because of behavioral, medical, or learning needs. However, the supplemental staff member should not

I never thought of it that way before?...

focus exclusively on the student with a disability but should assist the teacher with operating the class. Full-time support is often provided by a paraprofessional; it also may be provided by the special educator. Our experience suggests that a variety of adults rather than one person should provide support to a student throughout the day. For example, Melissa required full-time support during all her 6th grade classes. However, she had different support providers during each class period. That approach allowed Melissa to learn from various adults and guaranteed that her participation did not depend on one staff member's attendance. It also promoted classroom teachers' ownership of and responsibility for Melissa as their student rather than viewing Melissa as the support provider's student.

Ownership of student learning + Responsibility

Coteaching by general and special educators offers another way to deliver full-time support. Coteaching is an excellent way for general and special educators to become immersed in grade-level curriculum as they jointly develop and deliver lessons. The only real drawback of coteaching is that it is impossible to be in two places at one time. In other words, when students in a cotaught classroom receive special education support, students in the other classes do not. Consequently, other adult support models such as the following should also be available.

Scheduled Adult Support. When adult support is scheduled for specific activities or times of day, special education teachers and paraprofessionals plan their day to meet individual student needs and IEP goals. In this model, the general and special educators do not work together to plan all the curriculum for the class; instead, they develop specific lessons for the times the special supports are in class. That type of support is predictable and reliable and allows students to receive specialized instruction at points during the school day, while benefiting from increased peer interactions and opportunities for independence through natural supports during the rest of the day. For example, in Ivette's 5th grade class, the special educator arrives each day at 10:30, just as the classroom teacher begins guided reading groups, leaving other students to work in one of several learning centers. The special educator joins Ivette's learning center and supports all students. In Dwain's 6th grade class, a paraprofessional is scheduled into the final 10 minutes of mathematics class to assist

Dwain with recording his homework assignments. Dwain needs this small prompt from an adult, as do several other students who have trouble remembering their homework. Scheduled support does not have to look the same throughout the week. For instance, when Dwain's science teacher planned a special squid dissection lab in her class, she asked for additional special education support as a one-time scheduled event.

Intermittent Adult Support. Intermittent support involves drop-in checkups and responses to situations in which students suddenly require additional assistance. Special education teachers and paraprofessionals must have time to respond quickly to events as they arise. If all support team members are scheduled full time into specific classrooms, they have little flexibility to respond to the dynamic needs of the school. We suggest that throughout the day at least one member of the special education support team be unscheduled or "on call" and that this on-call responsibility rotate among specialized staff. For example, when Ivette's teacher decided to introduce a new assignment that she had not thought she would get to, an unscheduled special educator immediately helped modify the assignment for Ivette. When Dwain's science teacher decided to give a pop quiz, the paraprofessional who was on call went to the class to read the quiz aloud to Dwain. Special educators can also use intermittent support to appraise a student's participation, to observe peer interactions, to collect data on student progress toward IEP goals, to evaluate the performance of a paraprofessional, or to determine if less specialized support is required.

Supplemental Adult Support. An additional type of support involves related services personnel (i.e., speech and language specialist, physical therapist, occupational therapist, career counselor). Such supplemental support services should foster student participation in school activities and must be coordinated with the instructional schedule. Supplemental adult supports should not pull students out of critical class experiences or focus on isolated skills development. An example of well-coordinated supplemental support is when the speech and language specialist works in foreign language classrooms to provide additional instruction on speech sounds and communication skills, thereby benefiting students with and without disabilities through increased interactions with a knowledgeable adult.

Structured Peer Support. Peer support can be formally structured in many ways for any student. Structured peer support can be particularly valuable for newcomers to a school, English language learners, or those who are academically gifted but socially reserved. In all cases, peer supports broker both social and academic exchanges.

In some secondary schools, students have the option to take a class or to receive elective credit for serving as an academic mentor known as a peer tutor. Participating tutors receive on-the-job training, guidance, and feedback from supervising educators. They have graded performance expectations and assignments just as in any other class.

Many elementary schools also have organized peer support systems for peer helpers who rotate, usually by the week, to assist anyone who needs help. More formalized peer tutoring arrangements are also becoming commonplace. Cross-age tutors, trained and assigned to teach in the lower grades, are a powerful supplemental resource for teachers looking for extra instructional support for students with and without disabilities.

Natural Peer Support. The ultimate goal in providing personal supports is to fade adult and formalized supports while developing natural supports that are generically available in a classroom. Ivette is naturally supported during art class when a neighboring classmate helps her hold the paintbrush. Melissa receives natural support when teammates cue her to rotate her position during a volleyball game. Natural peer support looks different at different ages and in different contexts. However, the goal remains the same: support that occurs naturally. An important role of educators is to connect students and to facilitate natural support giving and receiving at every opportunity.

Summary

Palm Crest's three-year journey toward genuine inclusive educational practice taught us much of what is articulated elsewhere in this book. We believe that a few lessons bear repeating:

- To achieve inclusive educational goals, we needed to reconfigure how adults worked with one another and to be flexible and responsive in structuring adult and natural peer supports.
- Administrative support was key to creating an inclusive school community. Our principal listened when we proposed our plans each year and gave us time to perfect our practices.
- Success breeds success. As we got better at supporting students and fellow teachers, more students were welcomed into general education classrooms.
- Success begins small—in our case, with one classroom. Then we spread the word and expanded efforts schoolwide.
- We learned from and corrected mistakes. For instance, we undersupported or oversupported students and had only one fixed coteaching model. We could fix the problem by having a continuum of support options and being flexible in moving among students or classes.

When the staff at Palm Crest embarked on the path toward inclusion, we believed that the school motto—"Where miracles happen every day"—applied to students. We didn't expect to discover that it also applied to us, the adults. Inclusion allowed us to miraculously and continuously transform relationships, teaching practices, and perceptions of what was possible.

References

Fisher, D., Frey, N., & Sax, C. (2004). *Inclusive elementary schools: Recipes for success* (2nd ed.). Colorado Springs, CO: PEAK Parent Center.

Fisher, D., Frey, N., & Thousand, J. S. (2003). What do special educators need to know and be prepared to do for inclusive schooling to work? *Teacher Education and Special Education, 26(*1), 42–50.

McGregor, G., & Vogelsberg, R. T. (1998). *Inclusive schooling practices: Pedagogical and research foundations: A synthesis of the literature that informs best practices about inclusive schooling.* Baltimore: Paul H. Brookes.

Ogle, D. (1986). K-W-L: A teaching model that develops active reading of expository text. *The Reading Teacher, 39,* 564–570.

Chapter 6

Access to the
General Education Curriculum for All:
The Universal Design Process

Alice Udvari-Solner, Richard A. Villa, and Jacqueline S. Thousand

Let's examine three students—Shamari, Ivan, and Christina—in Ms. Chavez's 11th grade history class.

Shamari seems to succeed effortlessly in academic and extra-curricular venues: he's captain of the baseball team, a tennis player, and first trumpet in the high school band. Passionate about environmental issues, Shamari volunteers his opinions with confidence in public settings. He is opinionated about school politics and was elected to represent his peers at the school board. Shamari exhausted high school math and is taking advanced math at the university in the evening. Statistics, data analysis, technology applications, and Internet research are his strong skills. He recently helped establish a state-of-the-art Web site for the school. Shamari has shown ability in teaching others but does not like working in groups because he believes it is "communism in disguise."

Ivan arrived from Chechnya, where his family was killed in the Chechen civil war. Catholic charities assisted him in coming to the United States to live with his uncle, who is also a newcomer to this country and who recently lost his job. Ivan and his uncle are tempo-rarily residing in a homeless shelter. Ivan still has limited English pro-ficiency. However, he is motivated to communicate and seeks out other students with his approachable smile, curious disposition, and cooperative manner. Ivan draws pictures to communicate his ideas when words fail. He often carries a prized, out-of-date, 35mm camera plus pictures of his life in Chechnya as a social bridge to

134

initiate conversations with others. Ivan's teachers have noticed his interest in anything mechanical and his ability to solve technological problems by taking things apart. The art teacher has noticed his eye for detail and has taken him under her wing to create a mural in the cafeteria. One educational assistant speaks some Russian and, along with Ivan's uncle, helps translate for Ivan. Because of his unstable housing, Ivan frequently comes to school tired and has fallen asleep several times in classes.

Christina enjoys everything about being an 11th grader. Approaching each class with enthusiasm, she is known for her sense of humor and physical energy. Well liked by male and female friends, she has been described as empathetic in her relationships. Christina has Down syndrome. Because Christina's sight-word vocabulary currently stands at 100 words, one of her continuing challenges at the secondary level is to access and gain meaning through text. Although Christina is an emerging reader, she gains significant breadth and depth in concepts from conversations and visual presentations. Christina is eligible for special education services, and the goals in her Individualized Education Program (IEP) offer insight into her educational priorities. Her priority goals include (1) actively engaging in class activities and discussions by making relevant comments or asking questions; (2) writing short paragraphs with adult, peer, or technological support; (3) improving enunciation; (4) making a timely transition between classes by independently following her schedule; (5) learning a minimum of 10 core curriculum facts per month in each academic class; (6) respecting other people's property; (7) creating, dictating, and editing a school-related story each week; (8) participating in extracurricular activities of her choice; (9) developing work skills by engaging in community job placements; and (10) traveling independently in the community by walking or riding the bus to and from destinations.

A diverse class composition is not unusual; rather, it is the norm in today's multicultural and multilingual inclusive schools. What advice and tools can we give to Ms. Chavez to ensure that all 27 students, including the three just profiled, successfully engage with the curriculum in her history class?

Access to Curriculum Through
Universal Design Versus Retrofit

The term *general curriculum* is defined from a special education perspective in the U.S. *Federal Register* (1999, p. 1470) as "curriculum that is used with nondisabled children." The general curriculum, then, is the whole of the educational experiences typically afforded students without disabilities. This whole includes not only what we usually think of as curriculum (i.e., the curricular content) but also the processes and products associated with curriculum delivery and assessment.

Collectively, we have extensive experience working with teachers who work diligently to help students access the curriculum. We have often observed teachers struggling to retrofit or alter preexisting curriculum and instructional methods. In a retrofit scenario, educators find themselves developing accommodations and modifications for individual students who enter a preexisting educational situation where there are particular materials, a typical way of delivering instruction, and a typical way to assess students. That approach is similar to retrofitting buildings on or near fault lines or retrofitting buildings erected before federal wheelchair access requirements. Essentially, teachers solve problems after the fact in an attempt to fit a student into the existing framework.

An alternative to retrofitting is *universal design*. "Universal design is a concept that refers to the creation and design of products and environments in such a way that they can be used without the need for modifications or specialized designs for particular circumstances" (Fortini & Fitzpatrick, 2000). Curb cuts are an example of universal design. They are expensive to add after the fact but cost virtually nothing if designed in from the start. Curb cuts allow wheelchair access to sidewalks; they also ease stroller access and reduce the probability of joint stress for joggers and faulty footing for all sidewalk users.

What does universal design look like when applied to a school curriculum? Differentiated materials, methods, and assessment alternatives are considered and created in advance with the full range of students' differences in mind. The school makes readily available to teachers the books on tape and other alternative reading materials of high interest and multiple levels of difficulty. Teachers take advantage of natural peer supports and instructional technologies (described in this chapter and Chapter 5) that reflect best educational practices. They routinely use partner learning, cooperative group learning, integrated thematic units and lessons, and hands-on learning experiences. They take the community to the classroom and the classroom to the community as they incorporate service learning, the Internet, and other technology into learning opportunities. They use authentic assessment methods such as curriculum-based assessment, artifact collections and portfolios, individual learning contracts, and demonstrations. In summary, educators implement the three goals of universal design for learning (UDL) identified by Rose & Meyer (2002). The goals of UDL are to provide students with multiple means of *representation,* multiple means of *engagement,* and multiple means of *expression.*

Initiating a universal design approach requires educators to think about three distinct curriculum access points: content, process, and product. *Content* concerns what is taught or what we want students to learn, know, and do. *Process* concerns how students go about making sense of what they are learning. *Product* concerns how students demonstrate what is learned (Tomlinson, 1995a, 1995b). Those three access points directly reflect the three goals of universal design for learning. Specifically, content requires multiple representations of material to be learned, process requires multiple means for student engagement, and product requires multiple means for student expression of learning.

The rest of this chapter shows how to shift from retrofit to universal design for student diversity and curriculum access. This is not to say that curriculum retrofitting will never be needed. Sometimes a student–curriculum mismatch will not have been encountered before, so teachers will need to invent unique accommodations and modifications.

A Process for Universal Design of Content, Process, and Product

Given state and district curriculum standards and the demands of an increasingly diverse learner population, how can a teacher design meaningful learning activities to address the standards and educational needs of all students? How can a teacher minimize the need to retrofit lessons and units for students with disabilities and other differences? Is there a step-by-step process for designing lesson plans to maximize access to curriculum and learning? In response to these questions we offer the *Universal Design Process* as a systematic decision-making method for differentiation. Figure 6.1 illustrates the four primary design points of this process.

Design Point I: Facts About Students

For every educator, the process of differentiating curriculum and instruction begins by knowing your students. Developing positive profiles of students' social and academic abilities, strengths, and learning concerns is an essential first step; such "facts" about students can reveal pertinent strategies for effective teaching. A helpful framework for understanding and finding strengths in all students is the Theory of Multiple Intelligences (MI) by Howard Gardner (1983, 1997). Through his research, he concluded that intelligence had been defined too narrowly; intelligence is multifaceted. MI theory assumes that all students possess an array of the following intelligences that can be cultivated to emerge in unique configurations:

1. Verbal/linguistic—is word-oriented; is sensitive to the sounds, structure, meaning, and functions of words; may show affinity to storytelling, writing, reading, and verbal play (jokes, puns, riddles).
2. Logical/mathematical—is concept-oriented; has capacity to perceive logical or numerical patterns; has a scientific or experimental nature to discover and test hypotheses.
3. Visual/spatial—is image- and picture-oriented; is able to perceive the world visually and to perform transformations

Figure 6.1

Universal Design Points

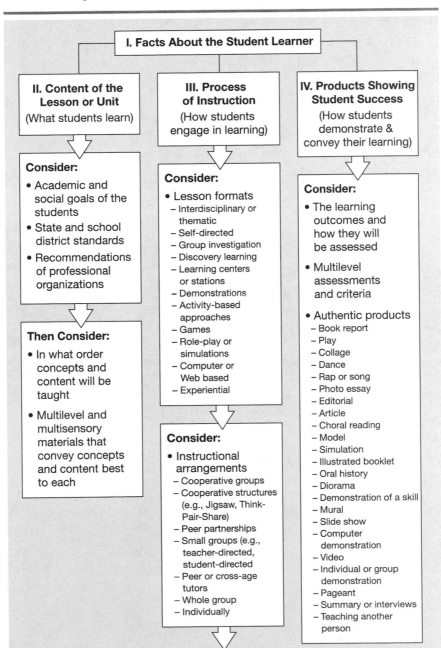

Figure 6.1 (continued)

Universal Design Points

III. Process of Instruction (Continued)

Consider:

- Social or physical environmental conditions or lesson location
  - With selected others
  - In specified classrooms
  - In another part of school building
  - In the community
  - With altered environmental factors (e.g., light, sound, physical access)
  - With changed or developed social rules

Pause and Reflect about specific students

Consider:

- Student-specific teaching strategies

Consider:

- Systems of support, assistance, or supervision

on those perceptions; may daydream and demonstrate artistic, designer, or inventive qualities.

4. Musical—is rhythm- and melody-oriented; can produce and appreciate rhythm, pitch, timbre, and multiple forms of musical expression; may be animated or calmed by music.

5. Bodily kinesthetic—is physically oriented; uses one's body movements for self-expression (acting, dancing, mime); excels in athletics; uses touch to interpret the environment; can skillfully handle or produce objects requiring fine-motor abilities.

6. Interpersonal—is socially oriented; has strong mediation and leadership skills; can teach others and discern moods, temperaments, and motivations of other people.

7. Intrapersonal—is intuitively oriented; can access and interpret one's own feelings; may be strong willed or self-motivated; may prefer solitary activities (Armstrong, 1994).

8. Naturalist—has capacity to classify nature; has outstanding knowledge of or sensitivity to things that exist in the natural world; has ability to discern patterns in nature (Checkley, 1997; Gardner, 1997).

Shamari's, Ivan's, Christina's, and other students' MI profiles (Figure 6.2) can be helpful to Ms. Chavez as she considers the potential materials and instructional processes she could use within a lesson or unit to capitalize on an individual student's strengths and intelligences; to cultivate nonstrengths, or intelligences that are less evident among students; and to optimize responsiveness from her 27 students with a wide spectrum of abilities.

Design Point II: Content

Content, the second design point, has multiple dimensions, including what is to be taught; what level of knowledge or proficiency students are to demonstrate; and what context, materials, and differentiation are necessary to allow all students, including those with disabilities, a point of entry to learning. (See Figure 6.1 for content considerations.)

Content is not formulated, selected, or delivered in a vacuum. Public policy and national and state standards have a huge influence

Figure 6.2

A Multiple Intelligences Framework for Viewing Student Abilities

Student	Areas of Intelligence	Description
Shamari	Verbal/linguistic	Expresses himself well verbally in public settings
	Logical/ mathematical	Excels in mathematics; enjoys data analysis; readily applies technology
	Visual/spatial	Has affinity for the computer, Internet searches, Web design
	Musical/rhythmic	Plays the trumpet well
	Bodily/kinesthetic	Plays tennis and baseball
	Intrapersonal	Formulates and expresses personal opinions; is self-driven
	Interpersonal	Is well liked by peers and was elected student representative; enjoys teaching others, but prefers to work alone rather than in groups
	Naturalist	Is passionate about environmental issues
Ivan	Verbal/linguistic	Is a non–English speaker learning a second language
	Logical/ mathematical	Is interested in anything mechanical, can solve technological problems by taking things apart
	Interpersonal	Readily approaches others in a cooperative and friendly manner
	Visual/spatial	Draws pictures to communicate; shows ability in photography and graphic arts
Christina	Verbal/linguistic	Has sight word vocabulary of 100 words; finds access to and meaning from secondary texts difficult; gains significant breadth and depth of information from conversations and visual presentations; possesses a sense of humor
	Visual/spatial	Reads with a sight word approach; gains information readily from visual presentations
	Intrapersonal	Is enthusiastic about school and life; is well-adjusted
	Interpersonal	Expresses empathy in relationships; is social with others

on content. For example, the call for high standards has become a national cry, which has been reinforced by the 2001 No Child Left Behind Act's requirements of accountability for all students' learning and the 1997 Individuals with Disabilities Education Act (IDEA) mandate for students' IEPs to ensure curriculum access. Students with disabilities are included in that call for high standards. Almost every state has adopted curriculum standards, frameworks, and assessment systems that drive the content decisions that teachers must make each day. Although state and district standards provide broad parameters for the content of a lesson or unit, the students' academic and social needs must be considered to create meaningful learning experiences from these broad guidelines. Facts about students' MI profiles, past learning experiences, prior knowledge, and current interests and abilities are invaluable in designing students' multilevel goals and objectives.

We want all students to acquire and use knowledge meaningfully. However, the scope and degree of mastery that we expect will vary across students. Within any lesson, unit, or classroom, there will likely be multilevel goals. For example, all students in a class may engage in the same curricular content but the focus may be more or less complex for each student. Students may address the same content but be required to use different response modes to demonstrate their knowledge (e.g., speak rather than write, point rather than speak). The teacher may require an increased or decreased rate of completing or pacing the content or have differentiated expectations about the level of mastery, degree of quality, or quantity of the curricular requirements. Finally, students may focus on similar content, but some may have more functional applications (Udvari-Solner, 1996, 1998).

Design Point III: Process

Process, the third design point, concerns instructional strategies that afford students multiple means of engaging with the curriculum. Over the past three decades, a tremendous amount of research has been conducted to determine effective instructional strategies to help students with disabilities access curriculum. Kronberg and York-Barr (1997) and McGregor and Vogelsberg (1998), for example, provide comprehensive reviews of such practices derived from general and special education research. Among the demonstrated organizational and instructional approaches are the use of (1) assistive technology, (2) positive approaches to support challenging behavior, (3) collaborative plans and coteaching among general and special educators, (4) ways to teach students "learning-to-learn" strategies, and (5) constructivist principles that help students discover and construct their own knowledge. Additional strategies (see Chapter 5 and the introduction to this chapter) include peer-mediated instructional arrangements such as partner and cooperative group learning, integrated cross-curricular thematic units, hands-on methods using realia (i.e., real objects), access to the Internet, service learning to connect school and community, and community-based projects.

In terms of lesson and unit planning, process requires decisions about (1) lesson formats, (2) instructional groupings, (3) the nature of the learning environment, and (4) specific decisions for some students about optimal teaching strategies and systems of support or supervision. The organizational design of a learning experience, or the lesson format, dictates how information is imparted to students and how they will interact with that content. Teachers may choose from many lesson formats (see the middle column of Figure 6.1). Because these formats allow for multisensory experiences and are more active and interactive, students who don't respond well to a traditional lecture/demonstration/practice orientation have more avenues to participation.

A related decision concerns methods of grouping students, or the learning configurations for structuring a lesson. Instructional arrangements dictate whether a student will work alone, function as part of a large group, or coordinate with a small number of classmates. As Tomlinson (1999) suggests, the key is to use a variety of instructional arrangements across a day or week for a calculated balance, including (1) large-group or whole-class instruction; (2) teacher-directed small-group instruction; (3) small-group learning; (4) one-to-one teacher-to-student instruction; (5) independent or individual work; (6) partner learning, peer tutors, or cross-age tutors; and (7) cooperative learning groups (Udvari-Solner, 1996).

Environmental conditions are another consideration when engaging students in learning. Where the lesson takes place; the physical arrangement of the room for individual students; and factors such as lighting, noise level, seating, and physical location and accessibility to learning materials are important environmental design decisions. The social rules observed in the classroom (e.g., hand-raising is required to answer a question) are also an integral part of the environmental conditions that set the climate and activity level and that guide acceptable interactions.

After considering the optimal lesson format, instructional arrangement, and environmental conditions, it is important to reflect on the lesson and to consider whether specific students may need unique support strategies. Teaching strategies are the explicit and implicit ways that an educator gives directions, cues, prompts, and corrective feedback; checks for understanding; questions; manages behavior; or provides physical assistance. Student-specific teaching strategies are techniques that go beyond the already structured technical aspects of delivering instruction. They may include strategies to connect the lesson's content to a particular student's culture, home, and community life (Udvari-Solner, 1996).

In a truly heterogeneous classroom, some students may need higher levels of assistance, intervention, or supervision than are typically provided to other students. Support needs may vary daily or be required at predictable times, but rarely does a student need continuous, one-to-one supervision. The amount and type of support needed for an individual student to meaningfully participate is a necessary design consideration. When added support is warranted, natural supports, or assistance that can be provided by the general education teacher and classmates, are preferable. Additional instructional staff members (e.g., a paraprofessional) may be needed at times, but should be implemented only with clear goals to fade assistance, teach students self-management, or model strategies that transfer the support back to the natural system of the classroom.

Design Point IV: Product

The fourth decision point determines what will be the product of students' learning, or how students will demonstrate and convey their learning. Product access, or assessment of learning outcomes, requires the development and use of multiple ways for students to express their understanding of the curriculum. Here, the notion of multiple intelligences again becomes important as a guide to thinking about the assessment, or the products of learning, in new ways. Falvey and colleagues point out that the question that educators and psychologists often struggle with is, "How smart is this student?" Gardner suggested that this is the wrong question. What needs to be addressed is, "How is the student smart?" This question presumes that all students are smart; they are just smart in different ways (Falvey, Blair, Dingle, & Franklin, 2000, p. 194).

An Example of the Application of Universal Design

Ms. Chavez teaches an integrated English and social studies course in a 90-minute extended block at O'Keefe High School. Among her 27 students are Shamari, Ivan, and Christina, who were introduced earlier in this chapter. As one of the first steps to introduce her new unit of study, Ms. Chavez told the students that they would be studying the Vietnam War and shared the following curriculum standards that must be addressed during their investigation:

1. Trace the origin and geopolitical consequences (domestic and foreign) of the Cold War and the containment of Communism policy (e.g., the Vietnam War).
2. Organize people and events according to chronology, geography, and theme to analyze similarities, differences, and relationships.
3. Use cause-and-effect arguments to demonstrate how significant events have influenced the past and present in the United States.
4. Identify significant events, people, and documents in major eras of U.S. history.
5. Evaluate, take, and defend positions on the influence of the media on U.S. political life.

6. Formulate questions about and defend analyses of tensions within a democracy (e.g., civil disobedience and the rule of law). (See California Standards at http//:www.cde.ca.gov/standards/history/grade11.html.) (Madison Metropolitan School District, 2003)

To solicit students' prior knowledge and to determine the direction that she and her students would take in this unit, Ms. Chavez engaged the learners in a modified K-W-L strategy by asking three questions (Carr & Ogle, 1987). K-W-L stands for Know, Want to Know, and Learned. The strategy requires students to use a three-column graphic organizer that illuminates what students currently know about a subject, what they hope to learn, and what new knowledge is gained ultimately through study. Ms. Chavez adapted the technique by asking students, "What do you want to know about the Vietnam War? How do you want to learn about the Vietnam War? How do you want to show me what you have learned about the Vietnam War?"

During the process, Ms. Chavez noted some weaknesses in her students' knowledge base. She asked them to continue thinking about the three questions for homework. In addition, she assigned a short passage to read that evening from the textbook and requested that they speak to their parents, other relatives, and neighbors about the war. The following day, Ms. Chavez and the students compiled the information about the content they wanted to learn, the processes they would use to learn about the Vietnam War, and the types of products they could produce to demonstrate their learning. The results are shown in Figure 6.3.

As a result of the modified K-W-L activity, Ms. Chavez developed a menu from which each student chose three methods to convey knowledge about the Vietnam War at the unit's end. In individual conferences, Ms. Chavez and each student reviewed the curriculum standards and the class-generated list of questions of interest to select a focus of each student's work. Students were to engage in at least one activity with a partner or group and to complete at least one activity alone. The menu for student choice is shown in Figure 6.4.

Figure 6.3

Modified K-W-L Strategy to Determine Focus of the Unit

Content (What do you want to know about the Vietnam War?)

STUDENT-GENERATED	TEACHER ADDITIONS
Why did we fight the war?	Was the war limited to Vietnam?
How long did it take us to win the war?	How were people selected to fight in the war?
Why didn't we win the war?	What was the cost of the war (e.g., fiscal, human loss, effect on other social initiatives in the United States)?
How many people died?	
What kinds of weapons were used?	
What was the effect of the war on their society and ours?	What role did the media play? Should they have done anything differently?
What role did music play, if any?	In what ways did we dehumanize the Vietnamese?
Why were so many people opposed to the war?	What effect, if any, did the Vietnam War have on public acceptance of subsequent U.S. military involvement?
What happened to people who refused to fight in the war?	
How did the war end?	How did the war affect U.S. and Vietnamese society?
Which countries were our allies and which were our enemies?	Does the United States have a relationship with the Vietnamese government today? Are there any unresolved issues?
What is Communism? Why was it considered bad?	
What kind of government does Vietnam have now?	How were veterans treated then compared to now?
What was it like to fight there?	How does Vietnam compare to other wars?
What is Agent Orange?	
How many other wars has Vietnam fought? Has it won all of them?	What dimensions of comparison are relevant?

SOURCES OR MATERIALS TO LEARN THIS INFORMATION	TEACHER ADDITIONS TO SOURCES OR MATERIALS
History texts	Books (e.g., *The Pentagon Papers*)
First-person narratives (written and person-to-person contacts)	Biographies (e.g., John McCain)
Content from the Internet, newspapers, books, political cartoons	
News programs, documentaries, and movies from that time and about that time (e.g., *The Deer Hunter; Good Morning, Vietnam*)	

Figure 6.3 (continued)

Modified K-W-L Strategy to Determine Focus of the Unit

Process (How do you want to learn about the Vietnam War?)
Work alone, with partners, cooperatively, or in small groups.
Work in learning stations with topics of interest to share resources and discuss ideas.
Read texts individually or discuss in group literature circles.
Interview people who fought in the war, people who favored the war, and people who were opposed to the war.
Conduct Internet and library research to review books and newspaper stories from the time.
Analyze and critique media from that era (e.g., political cartoons).
Engage in simulations and role-plays to understand perspectives of others.

Products (How do you want to show me what you have learned about the war?)
Give an oral report (e.g., presentation, debate).
Submit a written report (e.g., report, PowerPoint® presentation).
Make a visual presentation (e.g., drawings, posters, cartoon strips).
Create graphic and mathematical summaries that compare and contrast the United States and Vietnam across numerous dimensions (e.g., economic structure, resources, diversity of population, geography, military resources, allies, religions, imports and exports, political system).
Articulate a personal position in a persuasive way about whether the war should have been fought, whether nuclear weapons should have been used to end the war, etc.

How did Shamari, Ivan, and Christina participate in this unit? In the process of learning, Shamari used his musical/rhythmic, logical/mathematical, and naturalistic intelligences as vehicles to access the curriculum, participate in learning activities, and demonstrate his knowledge. Two learning goals were perspective taking and analysis of data. Consequently, for his product of learning, Shamari created a written report that explored the immediate and long-term costs of the Vietnam War. He wrote about the amount of money expended by the U.S. and Vietnamese governments, types and amounts of armaments used, lives lost, people left homeless,

Figure 6.4

Menu of Methods and Product Choices for Vietnam War Unit

Verbal/linguistic	Logical/mathematical	Visual/spatial
Oral presentation	Graph	Photojournalism
Debate	Chart	Posters
Interview	Time line such as time line of critical events	Murals
PowerPoint® presentation	Statistical analysis	Graphic art pieces
	Extrapolation of data	Graphic displays
Other:	Other:	Other:

Musical/rhythmic		Bodily/kinesthetic
Poetry		Dramatic presentation of a scene, concept, or critical issue
Rap		Debate
Analysis of music of the times	**Topic: Vietnam War**	Mime, gestures, and sign language
Original piece of music		Interpretive dance
Other:		Other:

Intrapersonal	Interpersonal	Naturalist
Fictional diary entries written from the perspective of a U.S. or Vietnamese soldier, draft dodger, conscientious objector, parent who has one child fighting in the war and one child protesting the war	Interviews with people holding different perspectives about the war	Examine the impact of the war on the environment and people (e.g., Agent Orange, land mines)
Other:	Other:	Other:

effect of the war on Vietnam's neighbors, and long-term effects of the war on health (e.g., Vietnam veterans who are homeless or in hospitals, effect of Agent Orange on the rate of birth defects in Vietnamese children), and the environment (e.g., the impact of spraying Agent Orange, number of children killed or injured by land mines during and since the war's end).

To strengthen Shamari's interpersonal skills, other students provided data that they collected during their research, and he created and presented graphs and tables to summarize his own and his classmates' research. Shamari used music-editing software in a second project when he digitized sound bites from songs and political speeches of the era to create original music that synthesized various perspectives.

Ivan's visual/spatial and interpersonal strengths, as well as his life experiences, shaped his selection of learning activities (i.e., process). Given his limited use of English and need to practice, his work alone was minimized. The teacher arranged for Ivan to accompany other students on interviews and to take digital pictures of the interviewees and their artifacts from the Vietnam conflict (e.g., medals, letters). Some men in the homeless shelter noticed Ivan working with his uncle on activities related to the Vietnam War, and they revealed that they were veterans. With the aid of his uncle, who speaks English, Ivan interviewed the homeless Vietnam veterans.

For Ivan's learning product, an educational assistant who could speak Russian provided interpretive services so Ivan could verbally present his interviews. Ivan also drew pictures to illustrate the effects of war. Through his graphic presentation, Ivan compared and contrasted the Vietnam War with his own experiences in Chechnya.

Christina's selection of relevant content, processes, and products was influenced by her interpersonal, musical/rhythmic, and verbal/linguistic strengths, as well as her empathetic nature. With the teacher's assistance, Christina developed interview questions for a Vietnam War veteran, a war protestor, and a Vietnamese émigré who had fled the country after the United States lost the war. Christina traveled by bus with a peer to conduct the first two interviews and independently to conduct the third. With the use of word prediction software and peer editing, she wrote a paragraph summarizing each of her three interviews. Excerpts from the interview with the Vietnamese émigré appeared as part of an article that Christina published in the school newspaper. She orally presented to her classmates the similarities and differences between the positions of the veteran, the protestor, and the émigré.

Another of Christina's projects involved listening to music from the era and identifying whether the songs expressed pro-war or antiwar sentiments. Christina identified specific words or phrases in the songs to justify her classifications.

While learning about the Vietnam War, Christina addressed six priority objectives in her IEP: (1) staying engaged in class activities and discussions by making comments or asking questions; (2) writing short paragraphs with adult, peer, and technological support; (3) improving enunciation; (4) learning a minimum of 10 core curriculum facts per month in each academic class; (5) creating, dictating, and editing a school-related story each week; and (6) traveling independently in the community.

Using the universal design process outlined in this chapter, Ms. Chavez designed instruction that effectively promoted active and meaningful participation for the full range of students in her class, including Shamari, Ivan, and Christina.

Summary

Access to the general curriculum is most readily available by providing services in the regular education classroom. We need collaborative opportunities to define and develop a vision in public education where all students, including students with disabilities, actively engage in learning and progress in the general curriculum. Access to the general curriculum must not be viewed as exclusively a special education concern; it is dependent on factors associated with regular education and the general curriculum. Therefore, all students benefit when the general education curriculum becomes more accessible. (Office of Special Education and Rehabilitative Services, 1999, C-1&2)

The preceding quote from the federal call for proposals for a National Center on Accessing the General Curriculum summarizes the rationale for universal access to curriculum: it has the potential to benefit all students, each with a unique learning style and history. However, to successfully engage in universal design requires particular beliefs, including the following:

- Teaching is a complex act because of the unique learning characteristics of each student.
- Differentiation is a natural part of curriculum development, delivery, and refinement and should not be perceived as an extra step or a process reserved for a select group.
- Teachers already differentiate curriculum offerings and instructional design; universal design simply shifts the priority to the learning needs and active participation of specific students (i.e., up-front rather than after-the-fact consideration).
- The initial effort and time to jointly design curriculum and instruction among general and special educators is both equitable and more efficient.
- Effective teaching for students with disabilities is substantively the same as effective teaching for all students, and it enriches and expands learning options (Castagnera, Fisher, Rodifer, & Sax, 1998).

Engaging in curricular and instructional differentiation is an act of change. Leo Buscaglia has said, "Change. It has the power to uplift, to heal, to stimulate, surprise, open new doors, bring fresh experience, and create excitement in life. Certainly it is worth the risk" (Utah's Project for Inclusion Web site, 2001).

The universal design decision-making process described in this chapter is intended not only to demystify the task of differentiation, but also to serve as a collaborative tool to facilitate dialogue for change in educational thought and practice to provide access to the general education curriculum for all children. We recognize that changing or refining our practices feels risky and, at times,

153

uncomfortable. However, this state of temporary imbalance generates the most creative solutions.

References

Armstrong, T. (1994). *Multiple intelligences in the classroom.* Alexandria, VA: Association for Supervision and Curriculum Development.

Carr, E. G., & Ogle, D. (1987). K-W-L-plus: A strategy for comprehension and summarization. *Journal of Reading, 21*(8), 684–689.

Castagnera, E., Fisher, D., Rodifer, K., & Sax, C. (1998). *Deciding what to teach and how to teach it: Connecting students through curriculum and instruction.* Colorado Springs, CO: PEAK Parent Center.

Checkley, K. (1997, September). The first seven . . . and the eighth: A conversation with Howard Gardner. *Educational Leadership, 55*(1), 8–13.

Choate, J. S., & Evans, S. (1992). Authentic assessment of special learners: Problem or promise? *Preventing School Failure, 37*(1), 6–9.

Diez, M., & Moon, J. (1992). What do we want students to know? . . . and other important questions. *Educational Leadership, 49*(8), 38–41.

Falvey, M. A., Blair, M., Dingle, M. P., & Franklin, N. (2000). Creating a community of learners with varied needs. In R. A. Villa & J. S. Thousand (Eds.), *Restructuring for caring and effective education: Piecing the puzzle together* (2nd ed., pp. 186–207). Baltimore: Paul H. Brookes.

Fortini, M., & Fitzpatrick, M. (2000). The universal design for promoting self-determination. In R. A. Villa & J. S. Thousand (Eds.), *Restructuring for caring and effective education: Piecing the puzzle together* (2nd ed., pp. 575–589). Baltimore: Paul H. Brookes.

Gardner, H. (1983). *Frames of mind: The theory of multiple intelligences.* New York: Basic Books.

Gardner, H. (1997). Are there additional intelligences? The case of naturalistic, spiritual, and existential intelligences. In J. Kane (Ed.), *Education, information, and transformation* (pp. 135–152). Upper Saddle River, NJ: Prentice-Hall.

Harry, B. (1992). An ethnographic study of cross-cultural communication with Puerto Rican–American families in the special education system. *American Educational Research Journal, 29*(3), 471–494.

Hock, M. (2000). Standards, assessments, and individualized education programs: Planning for success in the general education curriculum. In R. A. Villa & J. S. Thousand (Eds.), *Restructuring for caring and effective education: Piecing the puzzle together* (2nd ed., pp. 208-241). Baltimore: Paul H. Brookes.

Kronberg, R., & York-Barr, J. (1997). *Differentiated teaching and learning in heterogeneous classrooms: Strategies for meeting the needs of all students.* Minneapolis, MN: Institute on Community Integration (UAP), College of Education and Human Development, University of Minnesota.

Madison Metropolitan School District. (2003). Content standards and grade level performance standards: Social studies: History, time, continuity, and change. Available: http://www.madison.k12.wi.us/tnl/social00.html.

McGregor, G., & Vogelsberg, T. (1998). *Inclusive schooling practices: Pedagogical and research foundations.* Baltimore: Paul H. Brookes.

Office of Special Education and Rehabilitative Services (OSERS). (1999). *Request for proposals 84-324H, C-1 & 2.* Washington, DC: U.S. Department of Education.

Rose, D., & Meyer, A. (2002). *Teaching every student in the digital age: Universal design for learning.* Alexandria, VA: Association for Supervision and Curriculum Development.

Tomlinson, C. A. (1995a). Deciding to differentiate instruction in middle school: One school's journey. *Gifted Child Quarterly, 39*(2), 77–87.

Tomlinson, C. A. (1995b). *How to differentiate instruction in mixed-ability classrooms.* Alexandria, VA: Association for Supervision and Curriculum Development.

Tomlinson, C. A. (1999). *The differential classroom: Responding to the needs of all learners.* Alexandria, VA: Association for Supervision and Curriculum Development.

Udvari-Solner, A. (1996). Examining teacher thinking: Constructing a process to design curricular adaptations. *Remedial and Special Education, 17*(4), 245–254.

Udvari-Solner, A. (1998). Adapting curriculum. In M. Giangreco (Ed.), *Quick guides to inclusion 2: More ideas for educating students with disabilities* (pp. 1–27). Baltimore: Paul H. Brookes.

U.S. Federal Register. (1999, March 12). *Rules and Regulations, 64*(48).

Utah's Project for Inclusion Web site (2001). Available: http://www.usoe.k12.ut.us/sars/Upi/index.htm.

Everything About Bob Was Cool, Including the Cookies

Richard A. Villa

"Dr. Villa, I made Bob a promise. Now I know I won't be able to keep it. I feel really bad. I don't know if I can—or should—tell you about it," a student named Bubba said to me. Who is Bubba? Who is Bob? What was the promise, and why couldn't Bubba keep it?

Bob Comes to Winooski

I first heard about Bob in November 1987. Totyona, a former paraprofessional in the Winooski (Vermont) School District called to ask if her new foster child could go to school in Winooski. Because Totyona and her husband, Todd, both resided in Winooski, my answer, of course, was "Yes." Totyona needed to give me more information about Bob, a young man with multiple disabilities, including cerebal palsy. For the previous 14 years, he had lived with his mom and dad in a small town in northeastern Vermont. He had attended a special education class, and Totyona had been an educator in his class. In May 1987, Bob's mom became ill and was no longer able to care for her son. So Bob went to live in a residential medical and educational facility. Bob's initial stay was to be six weeks. But by the time Totyona called me, Bob had lived there for six months. With his mom still unable to care for him, his stay had been extended.

Although Bob couldn't communicate orally or using sign language, a communication board or other device, or a consistent smile or frown, I believe he did communicate his depression and sense of loss while in the residential facility. He lost 16 pounds—a significant weight loss for someone as thin and medically fragile as Bob.

Bob was the first student with severe disabilities to be integrated into the mainstream at Winooski. A great deal of time, energy, and planning went into his transition. Bob's natural parents and foster mother were part of the initial transition meetings. At the residential facility, we met with everyone who provided services for Bob. We observed and videotaped him. We then detailed a plan for his transition. Our goal was for Bob to attend school full time within six weeks. A team of educators from Winooski (a junior high science teacher, a special education teacher, a speech and language pathologist, a school nurse, and I as the special education administrator) visited the facility.

In retrospect, one of the most important transition activities was the immediate involvement of students. A special educator who became Bob's service coordinator and I visited every junior high classroom and spoke with the students and, in a sense, introduced Bob to them. We showed parts of a videotape of Bob and described what we knew about him, including his strengths and some of his needs. Even though we didn't know a great deal about him, we pretended to know even less. We asked the students to help us brainstorm and identify strategies and resources to support Bob in his new school.

The students were great! Their advice ranged from what kind of musical tapes and notebooks Bob should have so he'd "fit in" to where he should hang out to be "cool." In 1987, if you were a junior high student, the cool place to hang out was by the bike rack. Students asked many questions, including how we intended to grade Bob. It was clear to them that we would need to make some accommodations.

Laura, a junior high student who happened to be the daughter of the superintendent, was one who greatly anticipated Bob's arrival. I learned in a conversation with the superintendent that he had overheard his daughter speak to her friends about Bob's impending arrival with such excitement that he had thought Bob was some rock star or teen idol. Even though Bob had not yet been to the school, he was one of the most "popular" students. Everyone had the opportunity to plan for him and to get to know about him; everyone was talking about him and wanting to meet him in person.

Today, a visitor to the school would not be surprised to see a student with severe disabilities as a natural part of our student body. But in 1987, Bob was "different"—at least initially.

Building Bob's Supports

The team of adults who assembled to work with Bob after his arrival put an extraordinary amount of time and energy into the planning process. In the beginning, we seemed to have more questions than answers. We secured technical assistance from state and local resources, such as the statewide Interdisciplinary Team for Students with Intensive Needs (I-Team). Having Totyona, Bob's foster mother, as a member of Bob's core team was extremely valuable. As a former teacher of and now parent to Bob, she brought a dual perspective to his team and had a wealth of information, concerns, and ideas.

To respond to Bob's needs, both adults and students assumed new roles. For example, the speech and language pathologist found herself among the people who fed Bob at lunchtime. That role change allowed her to assess Bob's oral-motor skills, work with him on communication issues, and establish a relationship. Bob needed to be repositioned, moved from his wheelchair, and engaged in range of motion exercises daily. Some professional and paraprofessional staff members received training in handling and positioning techniques and range-of-motion activities so they could share the new job function.

In their new roles, students were recruited and trained as volunteer tutors to assist in Bob's educational program. A dozen or so classmates became his peer support network. As Bob's peer buddies and *Circle of Friends* (Forest & Lusthaus, 1989; Falvey, Rosenberg, Forest, & Pearpoint, 2000), they helped include Bob in nonacademic aspects of school (meeting Bob at the bus, getting him from class to class, encouraging and facilitating his attendance at after-school activities) and in the social life outside of school. Bob's network was very diverse. There were students who were very popular, students who were quiet, students who had the full range of academic talent or achievement, students who had siblings with disabilities. They were possibly the most diverse crew of kids you could imagine. They had lots of different interests, but all shared a common one—a concern for Bob.

Initially, Bob's team targeted three priority goal areas for Bob's Individualized Education Plan (IEP). Communication was the highest priority, with objectives to increase Bob's vocalizations and visual tracking ability, establish discrimination among things of importance in his environment, respond to his name, explore ways for him to indicate choice, and develop a switch that he could use to activate electronically assisted communication and other devices. A second goal area was socialization. Bob's team wanted him to be included in many social activities, to spontaneously interact with peers, and to develop relationships. Bob's health was another priority, specifically, gaining back the 16 pounds he had lost and maintaining or regaining his range of motion. Those goals were met during Bob's first year as a Winooski student.

Year 1—Snapshots of Bob's School life

How were the objectives for Bob's socialization, health, and increased communication integrated into the curriculum and instructional practices of our junior high school? To begin with, Bob's team used a matrixing procedure to examine the possible times, places, classes, and activities within the general education schedule at the junior high (e.g., academic classes, specials, teacher advisory period) during which Bob's IEP objectives might be directly or incidentally addressed. The team then developed a schedule, which, in Bob's first year, included science, math, physical education, social studies, library, technology education, computer, and teacher advisory classes.

Teacher Advisory

During the morning teacher advisory period, Bob would frequently work with some students by using a panel switch. If Bob hit the panel switch, a tape player would turn on and music would begin to play. The music was always chosen by the students with whom Bob was working. They encouraged Bob to use the panel switch, and when he did, their efforts were reinforced by the music they had selected.

Science Class

As a former junior high science teacher, I took great interest in observing what went on in Bob's science class. I discovered that, in many ways, some things never change. For example, one day the class was engaged in dissecting frogs. Some students really got involved in the activity, some found it "gross," and some took parts of the frog and wiggled them in front of someone else's face, resulting in giggles and screams.

I was fascinated to see Bob's participation. Students were working in cooperative learning groups of three at lab tables. Each group had a dissecting pan, a frog in the pan, and dissecting tools. I noticed that Bob's lab group had the frog in the dissecting pan, but that the group hadn't placed the pan on a lab table as the other groups had. Instead, the pan sat on the lap tray connected to Bob's wheelchair, and Bob's teammates were gathered around the tray doing their work.

A couple of other objects also sat on the lap tray, including the blue cup that Bob used to drink water and juice. During the course of the activity, Bob's teammates would occasionally ask, "Bob, do you want a drink?" or "Bob, can you look at the blue cup?" Bob's response to the question was recorded by an instructional assistant who sat to the side. She was not directly involved in the activity but was always available to support Bob or any other student. The students were well aware of Bob's objectives regarding object discrimination and choice making, and they easily incorporated them into the dissection activity. Another of Bob's objectives, increased vocalizations, was also realized. Bob laughed and squealed as readily as any student when a teammate held up a part of the frog and wiggled it in his face. The experience clearly illustrated how students aptly involved Bob in planned activities, enabling him to address his objectives while simultaneously working on their own.

Mathematics

Bob also participated in math class. What did Bob and math have in common? Recall that visual tracking was one of Bob's communication objectives. That is, we wanted Bob to increase his ability to follow movement with his eyes. The math teacher had a booming voice and paced around the room. We found that by positioning Bob in such a way that he could see the teacher, Bob's eyes followed the teacher. We even began to see his head move. The teacher used Bob's and other students' names in word problems as he started each class. For example, after the class had studied the relationship of the radius, diameter, and circumference of a circle, the teacher asked, "Given the radius of the tires on Bob's wheelchair and the distance from this room to the cafeteria, how many revolutions would it take to get Bob from here to the lunch room?" The students measured, computed, and checked their answers by wheeling Bob to the cafeteria. Activities like this allowed us to see if Bob recognized his name—and allowed Bob to be a meaningful part of the classroom community.

In the second half of math class, the teacher usually engaged in whole-group direct instruction or assigned individual seat work. During that time, Bob could work on other IEP goals, go to lunch early (because he needed an extended time to eat), or work with a peer tutor or an instructional assistant on alternative objectives outside the class or in the community.

Social Studies

Bob's social studies teacher typically began class with Vermont stories, an activity that involved students coming to the front of the room and briefly presenting newsworthy happenings. They were encouraged to report about events in Vermont but were free to report about national, world, or personal events. I observed the class on Bob's day to report the news. Bob was wheeled to the front and the instructional assistant explained a new communication experiment with Bob. She placed a large piece of Plexiglas® verti-cally in front of Bob. It had a symbol for "Yes" in the upper right cor-ner and a symbol for "No" in the upper left. She then asked Bob a question, requesting him to look at the symbol (yes versus no) that indicated his preference. She repeated this technique with students asking questions. In the same amount of time it took for any class-mate to tell a Vermont story, the students became knowledgeable of Bob's new communication program and encouraged Bob to use the device throughout the day. From my observation of body language, the students were much more attentive to Bob's Vermont story than they were to stories presented by other classmates.

Physical Education

Where do most students have their physical development and edu-cation needs addressed? The same place that Bob's adaptive physi-cal education took place—the gym. If you visited Bob's gym class, you'd see him being repositioned and doing range-of-motion exer-cises on a floor mat. During a wrestling unit, Bob was joined on the floor by a lot of other students. During baseball season, he went out-side whenever his classmates were outside. Bob was a designated base runner for his team. When his batting partner hit a ball, Bob was wheeled quickly around the bases. I can still hear Bob laughing as he went from first base to second, to third, and home.

Year 2—Entrepreneurship and Social Life

By the start of Bob's second year, his 8th grade year, his family and support team began to ask questions about what was going to hap-pen to Bob after high school. Vocationally oriented goals were included in his IEP.

Budding Entrepreneurs

After some brainstorming, Bob's team came up with the idea of form-ing a small cookie production and sales business with three other classmates who had an interest in entrepreneurship. The business became known as Cota's Cool Cookies—"Cota" because that was

Bob's last name and "Cool" because the secret ingredient was cool mint and chocolate chips. Bob was the chief executive officer and head chef. By using his panel switch, Bob could turn on a beater that mixed the cookie batter. The other students in the business baked, packaged, and distributed the cookies. Cota's Cool Cookies was a collaborative enterprise that involved many other students in the school. Students in business class set up contracts and maintained the books for the business. Students in the art classes participated in a contest to design the product label. Cota's Cool Cookies were sold in the district's schools and in two neighboring school districts during lunch. They were also sold at the National Guard Armory, Winooski City Hall, and many other places in the community. Despite the numerous supplies that had to be purchased, Bob and his business partners turned a profit within a couple of months.

Life Outside of School

Bob's involvement with his peers extended beyond the school day. I remember Bob's foster mother, Totyona, saying, "I used to think it would be great if Bob had some friends coming over after school. Well, they came, and do you have any idea what it is like to have half a dozen junior high school–aged kids in your house all day—with all that energy?"

I will never forget the day when a teacher said to me, "I think Bob's going to be in a fight." I found that quite interesting and I said, "Wait a minute; tell me more." She explained, "You see, Bob has been invited to the Halloween dance by a cheerleader, and her ex-boyfriend, who is on the football team, is not too happy. He says he's going to pound Bob's face. What are we going to do?" We decided to do what we would do for any other student. We monitored the situation and followed the policy of not intervening unless absolutely necessary. After all, changing boyfriends and girlfriends is a part of normal adolescent development. Bob didn't get into a fight with the football player, and he did go to the dance—dressed as Beetlejuice and doing wheelies on the dance floor with his classmates.

Transitions

Toward the end of Bob's 8th grade year, Totyona notified the school that Bob would be moving with his foster family to a neighboring town and new school district. The members of Bob's support and friendship circle were saddened by the news, as were the teachers, the principal, and I. Before Bob came to Winooski, everyone wondered how he was going to fit in. Would he be accepted and appreciated for his individuality? I remember a teacher wondering, "Is he just going to sit in the back of my room, drooling, making noises, and disrupting my class?" Then he got to know Bob. Six months later, that same teacher said, "He has had such a powerfully positive influence on the students in junior high class. Can he please stay in my class another year?" I reminded the teacher of our school's adherence to the principle of age-appropriate placement. Bob needed to move along the grades with his peers.

Students in Bob's peer support circle, recalling their involvement in planning for his arrival 18 months earlier, demonstrated their knowledge of the importance of transition planning. Several classmates approached the administrators and requested to go to the school that Bob would be attending in the fall so they could facilitate his smooth transition. They wanted to be sure both students and staff knew what Bob could do and how they could support him. Bob's new school was contacted in late May and the special educator responsible for his program promised to get back to us. After summer break, some students were asked to come and speak with Bob's new classmates and teachers. In October, three students went, and the effect of their words and advocacy for their friend was evidenced in the thank-you letter from Bob's new school.

> Moriah Gosselin and Jason Messick spoke to Bob's afternoon classes. They spoke articulately and with humor and covered many important aspects of Bob's integration at your school. Most important was the regard and fondness for Bob evident in their presentations. They were excellent.

Chandra Duba, who came to school at 7 a.m. to speak with Bob's morning classes, discussed not only Winooski's experiences with Bob but also her own experiences with handicapped siblings.

Although Bob was the focus of their work, the effect of those young people went far beyond Bob. The attitudes and behaviors they modeled were lessons for us all about friendship and mutual respect. What they taught made the way easier for many handicapped students here. (K. Lewis, personal communication, November 20, 1989)

Early in December, Winooski students went back to see how Bob was doing. They excitedly reported that Bob looked great, seemed happy, and had a whole new peer support network. That Saturday, I spoke with Bob's foster parents. They were happy with Bob's transition and his emerging new support group.

On Sunday of the same weekend, while sitting at the breakfast table with his foster family, Bob suddenly died. He had contracted an undetected pneumonia that was too much for his fragile system to handle.

On Monday, I delivered the news. In all my years in education, the hardest thing I have had to do was gather Bob's Winooski classmates and tell them that their friend had died. Many students wanted to go to Bob's funeral, so the school arranged for a bus to take staff members and students on the two-hour trip to Bob's funeral.

As I sat in that funeral parlor and looked around, any doubts that I might have had about the benefits of inclusive education disappeared forever. I recalled funerals that I had attended for other students who had died, students who had been educated apart from their neighborhood peers. Those funerals usually were attended only by the family and other adults. It seemed to me that, in many ways, their lives had been anonymous. In contrast, this room was filled with children—the diverse group of Bob's peers who now were mourning the loss of a friend. Bob had not lived an anonymous life. He had died with dignity, respect, and friendship.

After the funeral, the bus ride home was silent. Then, little by little, students began to tell stories, amusing anecdotes, and remembrances about Bob. One student recalled playing a joke on a substitute teacher when he turned his back by taking Bob in his wheelchair and disappearing. Another student recalled the superintendent expressing concern about liability because Bob was being wheeled so quickly around the baseball diamond and athletic fields. They said that they didn't care if they had gotten into trouble with the superintendent; just hearing Bob laugh as he rounded the bases was worth the risk.

Staff members recalled how much planning had gone into Bob's initial integration into Winooski and how much they had learned from the experience that subsequently benefited other students. We discussed how much we had known intuitively about how to meet Bob's needs. We reflected on how Bob's presence taught students and adults alike to accept and appreciate the differences in others and themselves. We talked about the future. What if one of Bob's classmates became the parent of a child with a severe disability? Would having known Bob and his zest in life make a difference for that parent? Bob's classmates are the employers of the future. When approached with the prospect of hiring somebody like Bob, they might recall all that Bob was capable of doing and choose to employ that person.

It was at that point that Bubba, a star football, baseball, and hockey player, approached me with his dilemma. I encouraged Bubba to say what was on his mind, and he finally did. Bubba had promised Bob that when the two of them turned 21, they were going to go out and get rip-roaring drunk together. Clearly, drinking may not be what we want students thinking about, but many students do anticipate "becoming legal." For me, Bubba's confession was symbolic of a fundamental goal of inclusive schooling. You see, Bubba did not regard Bob as a "disabled person." Bubba saw Bob as Bob, a friend. What Bubba dreamed about for the two of them was no different from what he and other teens dream and scheme about, and Bob was part of it all.

Guidance personnel supported Bob's peers in finding ways to express their grief. Some students wrote in journals, others spoke with counselors, and others collected money to donate something in Bob's name and memory. Some students expressed anger and frustration at anyone who prevented a student like Bob from attending their school.

Advocacy Lives On

Shortly after Bob's death, a unique opportunity for advocacy came along that helped some students deal with their emotions. I had become aware of a girl in Canada, Becky Till, who was 14 years old, the same age as Bob. Like Bob, she had cerebral palsy and lived with a foster family (who eventually were able to adopt her). Becky's foster parents wanted her to attend their community's local school rather than the special school. Despite four years of advocacy efforts, they had yet to win Becky's access to the school. We made Winooski students aware of the opportunity for advocacy, and several wrote to the Ministry of Education of Ontario and the school board members of Becky's town, explaining why Becky belonged in school.

To mount further pressure, Becky's mother put on a conference in New Market, Ontario. She invited me and other disability rights advocates to speak. Although my words might be helpful, I knew it would be more important for the audience to hear students' words. Two of Bob's friends, Bubba and Moriah, traveled to Ontario and articulated their own and their classmates' views as to why Bob and Becky belonged in school. When asked why Bob belonged in public school, they responded simply, "Because he is human." They spoke of the benefits to all students of being educated together. Bubba expressed emotionally, "Nothing hurts more than losing someone you love." The students were strong and moving in their message, as reflected in the Sunday *Toronto Sun* headline, "Bubba Tells Becky, Fight Until You Win!"

It has been more than a decade since Bob's death, but in Bob's short time on earth, he touched my life and the lives of others in a profound way that lives on. He demonstrated for us the value of collaboration, inclusive education, friendship, and saying "Yes" to the unknown. He is fondly remembered.

Everything about Bob was cool, including Cota's Cool Cookies.

References

Falvey, M., Rosenberg, R., Forest, M., & Pearpoint, J. (2000). Building connections. In J. S. Thousand, R. A. Villa, & A. I. Nevin (Eds.), *Creativity and collaborative learning: The practical guide to empowering students, teachers, and families* (2nd ed., pp. 347–368). Baltimore: Paul H. Brookes.

Forest, M., & Lusthaus, E. (1989). Promoting educational equality for all students: Circles and MAPs. In S. Stainback & W. Stainback (Eds.), *Educating all students in the mainstream of education* (pp. 42–58). Baltimore: Paul H. Brookes.

Chapter 7

Questions, Concerns, Beliefs, and Practical Advice About Inclusive Education

Richard A. Villa, Jacqueline S. Thousand, Emma Van der Klift, Jonathan Udis, Ann I. Nevin, Norman Kunc, Paula Kluth, and James W. Chapple

> There are no foolish questions and no man becomes a fool until he has stopped asking questions.
>
> —Charles Steinmetz

This chapter consists of 15 questions and corresponding answers. We have tried to address educators' concerns with respect and to identify underlying beliefs. Many unfounded stereotypes about people with disabilities have risen out of popular "wisdom." Such beliefs might be based on lack of information, misinformation, or even myth. A teacher who has never taught a student with a disability, for example, might worry about behavioral issues because of seeing media representation. Some people might worry about "catching" a disability that they believe is contagious. Others might believe that people with disabilities are more fragile than their nondisabled peers. Each belief might or might not be true with certain individuals in certain circumstances. Left unquestioned, though, such beliefs can influence our behavior—often in negative or exclusionary ways—when relating to people we encounter in our schools and communities.

We don't pretend to have definitive answers or a corner on what is politically correct. The following comments represent our collective best thinking and are part of a dialogue that we hope will be ongoing and will include many voices in the future.

1. Many parents of children with disabilities do not believe that their children's needs can be met in general education. They expect a choice about placing their child in a classroom, resource room, special class, or special school. Does inclusion eliminate parental choice?

Conflict often exists between what parents believe is the best educational setting for their child and what the school offers. That conflict is acted out in various arenas besides special education. Some parents object to standards-referenced education, cooperative group learning, or other innovative teaching or assessment approaches.

In many noninclusive school communities, parents do not have a choice for supports in the local classroom because the supports are available only in separate places such as resource rooms or special classes. Inclusive policies and practices are not intended to eliminate parental and child choice. There will always be private alternatives to public education, and parents may choose placements other than their local community schools. Inclusive educational policies and practices simply make it possible for a child's educational placement of first choice to be the local school and community.

Parents' underlying concern is for their child's success. Their belief that their child will not be successful in general education is grounded in historical cases where supports were *not* provided. When special and general education personnel and resources are melded, best teaching practice and needed support increase dramatically along with student success. Further, because the 1997 reauthorization of the Individuals with Disabilities Education Act (IDEA) mandated that students with disabilities have access to general education, school systems and teachers are obliged to use educational practices that differentiate content, instruction, and assessment so each child can be successful in general education. Given those improvements in educational practice and law, families should see less need for separate programs and alternative choices. Regardless of parental choice, schools have a legal obligation to ensure that students with disabilities have an opportunity to be educated beside children without disabilities.

2. Isn't general education inappropriate for some children? Are inclusion advocates suggesting that the federal law be changed and the continuum of placement model discarded?

A defining characteristic of an inclusive school is a "zero reject" (Lilly, 1971) philosophy. Thus, when a discussion of inclusive education begins by identifying which groups of children (e.g., medically fragile, behavioral challenges) cannot "make it," we miss the point. Albeit largely unintended, the categorical (or individual) exclusion of children causes peers to wonder, "If my school can exclude them, what would make it exclude *me*?" Educators and others have increasingly recognized that a solid sense of belonging is a prerequisite to excellence and quality in education (refer to the *Circle of Courage* in Chapter 3).

Another reason it is dangerous to make decisions based on labels is related to beliefs and prejudices of the placement team. Teachers (and families) often make assumptions based on perceptions about what a student can and cannot achieve. We believe labels but are wrong about students and their potential. For example, throughout history, people assumed various populations who behaved differently were unable to learn, including those with cerebral palsy, autism, and deafness (Crossley, 1997). Educators have made damaging negative assumptions about the learning potential of girls, students of color, and students who speak English as a second language.

Inclusive education commits to every child and that child's differing needs. Thus, a constellation of services is taken to the child rather than the child being taken to the services, which makes more sense than a continuum of placement approach that removes children from the learning community. Ideally, an inclusive school provides supports within general education environments.

The question of student placement—what learning environment results in meaningful learning—and parent choice are closely linked. For some students with disabilities, the "regular" classroom may not be optimal, but it also may not be best for students *not* identified as disabled. Specifically, in 13 or more years of public schooling, it is unlikely that every teacher whom a student encounters will have all characteristics (e.g., content mastery, instructional skills, flexibility, warmth, compassion) that a parent wishes for a child. Although the dream is a perfect match every year, the reality is that most matches are only satisfactory. The nightmare is a very poor match.

A first step when planning for student differences is to identify the characteristics, skills, strategies, and knowledge that each student brings to different learning tasks and to identify likely educational mismatches. The next step is to determine how best to deliver the instruction, supports, and resources for particular settings. Fortunately, the response to individual student differences has mushroomed over past decades because of increased competence and technology, and more and more inclusive schools exist in the United States and Canada. As better and better educational experiences support and include all children, the concept of continuum will become less and less relevant. In other words, "placement" decisions and determinations about what constitutes a least restrictive environment will become moot points as communities embrace an inclusive educational philosophy and teach children together rather than apart. Segregated placements will fall by the wayside.

There clearly are students for whom a traditional "12 years of 185 7-hour school days does not constitute the 'magic formula' for learning" (Villa, Udis, & Thousand, 2002, pp. 151–152). For example, some children may desire and benefit from experiences and relationships that typically do not exist within the classroom walls or school building. To illustrate, a child may participate in an off-campus counseling group (e.g., for children who have been sexually abused) or employment training in a local business. Another child experiencing emotional difficulties may, for a time, need an altered school day that starts and ends on a flexible schedule and includes work and community service opportunities. Yet another student may need a temporarily shortened day and a mentor relationship with a respected community member during a period of extreme stress. Still others may need year-long support that includes a summer program to facilitate "staying out of trouble" in the community.

3. Many people in the deaf community do not believe the educational needs of children who are hard of hearing or

deaf can best be met in general education classes. How do you address their concerns and desire to immerse their children in deaf culture? Don't parents, advocates, and persons who are deaf or hard of hearing know what is best?

As with all students, children who are deaf use language to build mental constructs that serve as a foundation for future learning. Unlike children who can hear, children who are deaf learn language visually—in other words, sight comes before sound. Thus, sign language is, by far, the most accessible language to children who have been deaf from birth. Their learning can be seriously jeopardized if the acquisition and mastery of sign language are delayed by oral training. The deaf community has been understandably tenacious in stressing that students who are deaf must attend schools where sign language is the primary language of instruction. Failure to do so can compromise the comprehension and appreciation of the curriculum.

Some school districts have attempted to address such concerns by pulling out children for instruction, assigning interpreters to classrooms, and teaching sign to all children. Although those strategies appear to address the problem, many adults who are deaf worry that they are not nearly enough. Members of the hearing community, however well intentioned and enthusiastic in trying to learn American Sign Language, may not learn enough "sign as a second language" to provide real conversational stimulation to a student using sign. Consequently, such students may be prevented from experiencing the complexity and richness of sign language in course instruction and social interactions.

Nevertheless, the current education system has serious problems for children who are deaf or hard of hearing. Most programs are in regional or magnet schools, which are located in only a few places throughout the country. Children are often required to live apart from their families to attend. Advocates for inclusion worry that an educational system that forces people to choose between family life and school is seriously problematic. In addition, segregated schooling typically fosters a life that continues to be segregated from the community at large.

The question seems to be whether we, as a society, need to resign ourselves to the idea that a segment of our population must live apart. At the very least, we must try to find bridges that can link the hearing and nonhearing worlds. We must also continue to explore ways in which schools can restructure so students with different languages (i.e., oral and sign) can learn as a common community. When families make such a choice, the job of teachers and administrators is to ensure that (1) the choice does not interfere with a child's acquisition and mastery of sign as a first language, if that is the preferred language; (2) opportunities are available inside and outside school so children can interact with others who use sign as a first language and who otherwise positively identify with deaf culture, if they choose; and (3) aspects of the deaf culture are brought into the total culture of the school.

> 4. Advocates of inclusion appear to be opposed to any
>   homogeneous grouping. How are the needs of children
>   identified as gifted and talented going to be met in gen-
>   eral education classrooms? Those children shouldn't be
>   held back or be expected to teach other children, because
>   they are the leaders of tomorrow.

Inclusion advocates are not categorically against homogeneous grouping. They understand, however, that no two learners are the same and that grouping of any kind should be short-term and for specific, focused instruction. Educators are increasingly aware that intelligence is neither a unitary ability nor fixed in time. Among emerging conceptualizations is the idea that people possess "multiple intelligences" (Gardner, 1983, 1993; Checkley, 1997). (See Chapter 6 for more about multiple intelligences [MI] theory.)

Learning environments must be structured to nurture those differing intelligences. The label of "gifted and talented" takes on new meaning when thought of broadly (i.e., a student who excels in auto mechanics, computer science, art, or interpersonal intelligence is "gifted") rather than narrowly (i.e., a student who scores high on intelligence tests is "gifted"). Teachers who subscribe to an MI way of thinking about gifts and talents tend to respect all learning styles and to provide differentiated curriculum, a range of activities, and various ways for students to express knowledge and expertise.

Current gifted and talented education (GATE) programs expressly celebrate and support the talents of a few and have perpetuated racial and socioeconomic segregation, as evidenced by the gross underrepresentation of minority and poor Americans in GATE programs. In contrast, inclusive education acknowledges everyone's gifts and talents and helps all children reach their potential through the very educational experiences that were afforded only through GATE programs: active, constructivist learning; opportunities for in-depth and prolonged study of a special interest area; opportunity for mentorships and other community experiences; use of computers and other technology; and access to coursework in community colleges, businesses, and universities. Such experiences would continue to be available to former GATE students while now also available to all. These good educational practices should be an integral part of an inclusive classroom experience.

Former GATE students can benefit greatly from the instructional strategies (e.g., differentiated instruction and curriculum, peer-mediated instruction such as peer tutoring and cooperative learning) used by inclusive educators in response to student diversity. Specifically, peer-mediated teaching arrangements counter the lack of tolerance of others and the individualistic, competitive work styles that some students develop in GATE programs. Further, when strategies are implemented well (i.e., with each student having individualized outcomes and tasks for contributing to a partnership effort), all students achieve success and benefit by (1) engaging in higher-order thinking skills as they organize their thoughts and plan how to effectively communicate material and ideas to their partners in learning, and (2) simultaneously developing the interpersonal leadership skills (e.g., trust building, communication, problem solving, conflict resolution) necessary for the cooperative workplace and world of tomorrow.

Inclusive schooling does not mean that children with gifts and talents will not receive focused attention in either one-on-one or homogeneous group arrangements. On the contrary, both will be options, as needed, for any student. Capitalizing on the MI notion of human difference and potential, homogeneous groups could be arranged along with dimensions of interest or "intelligence" (e.g., musical preferences, recreational interests). Homogeneous "ability" grouping should occur only under clear conditions (Slavin, 1987), such as when grouping measurably reduces student differences for the targeted skill or concept, when teachers closely monitor student progress and change groupings as students progress, and when teachers actually vary their instruction from one group to the next. However, students should spend most of their school week with a heterogeneous peer group.

> 5. Are inclusion advocates concerned primarily with socialization? Aren't academics being sacrificed?

Academics, socialization, social and emotional development, life skills, employability skill development, and recreation are just some areas of concern when planning for a child's individualized program. None, including academics, should be ignored or viewed as the only potential priority area for a child with an Individualized Education Plan (IEP) or for any child. When we acknowledge that not every student must have the same objectives during an activity or lesson, any and all areas can be addressed. Furthermore, as many state standards articulate, academics are important—but primarily as vehicles to enable children to achieve vital results as good communicators, reasoning problem solvers, responsible citizens in a global society, and nurturers of themselves and others. Educational futurists predict that these vital results will be the most important for negotiating and surviving the rapid changes of 21st century life.

It is unwise to inadvertently set up an either/or choice between academics and socialization in school. First, current best instructional practices (see Chapter 5) and theories of learning such as constructivism teach us (and children understand) that learning is a constructed process that requires a social interaction component. Second, socialization—cooperation, collaboration, and developing relationships—can boost academic learning. Students learning to speak, write, and read often do best when around students who engage them in conversations throughout the day. Students learning to use technology and computers pick up those skills more quickly with help from other students who play games, send e-mail, or work cooperatively on a Web design project.

To illustrate, in their study of students with significant disabilities, Kliewer and Biklen (2001) found that the social and complex nature of the inclusive classroom gave students critical opportunities to gain literacy skills. For example, Rebecca, a "primarily nonspeaking" 5th grade student with autism, was considered "preliterate" by the professionals who had evaluated her. Determined to include Rebecca in classroom life, the classroom teacher had students brainstorm ways to engage Rebecca throughout the day. Some girls thought of passing notes (the kind that students typically give to each other during class to socialize). Once students started passing notes to Rebecca, unfolding them for her, and then reading them to her, the teachers noted Rebecca's obvious interest and nodding responses to notes such as, "Do you like James—yes or no?" As a result, Rebecca's teaching team constructed a "yes" or "no" response board and created a range of literacy experiences that were spin-offs of the initial note-passing experience (Kliewer & Biklen, 2001).

6. What is a child with severe disabilities going to do in a 9th grade science course?

This question is really asking why a student who has very different objectives from most class members would be included in an activity or class that does not, at first glance, seem to relate to that student's needs. Sometimes people don't realize just how rich a general education environment is, particularly for a student with intensive challenges. The variety of people, materials, and activities is endless and provides an ongoing flow of opportunities for communication and human relationship building, incidental learning in areas not yet targeted as priority objectives, and direct instruction in a student's high-priority learning areas.

Key to a student's meaningful participation is creative thinking by the student's support team—and the team always has at least four options for arranging a student's participation in general education activities. (1) A student can engage in the same activities as everyone else (e.g., practice songs in music class). (2) Multilevel curriculum and instruction can occur. That is, all students are involved in the same curriculum, but they are pursuing varied objectives at multiple levels according to their unique needs. For example, math students may be applying computation skills at varying levels—some with complex word problems, others with one-digit subtraction problems, and yet others with materials that illustrate counting with correspondence. (3) Curriculum overlapping involves students working in the same lesson but pursuing objectives from different curricular areas (see "Voice of Inclusion: Everything About Bob Was Cool, Including the Cookies"). (4) Alternative activities may be needed in a child's schedule to allow for community-based or work options or to address management needs (e.g., catheterization in the nurse's office). Alternative activities may also be considered when a general education activity cannot be adapted. Such parallel activities should mirror the instructional activity that is taking place in the classroom.

Extreme caution is advised in ruling an activity "impossible to adapt" or the general education classroom as inappropriate for a student with severe disabilities. We have learned through experience that general education (e.g., science class for Bob) can meet the needs of children with severe disabilities if adults and children in the school and greater community think creatively and collaborate. Theory and techniques now exist to empower and equip educators to adapt instruction for any student, including one with a severe disability (see Chapters 5 and 6).

> 7. How do we grade students with disabilities? Is it fair to give them an A or B for doing work that is significantly different from that of their classmates or after we have provided accommodations and modifications?

We recognize that a diploma or a grade in and of itself tells nothing about what a child knows, believes, or can demonstrate because of the variability within and across schools. For example, within a particular school, an earned grade in one math class may not mean the same as the same grade in another math class (e.g., calculus versus general math). In fact, within the same class, the learning of two students receiving the same grade could be vastly different. Many traditional grading practices and procedures are arbitrary and subjective. In any discussion about grades, we must first ask, "What is the purpose of grading? Is it to compare one student to another or to compare a student's performance to an outcome or a standard?" With an answer, we can devise more appropriate methods of student evaluation and assessment.

The "correct" approach to student assessment is a hotly debated issue. Some educators advocate the continuation of competitive, normative comparison practices. Others advocate adopting outcomes-based assessment (and instructional) strategies. The National Center on Education Outcomes, for instance, has called for identifying outcomes and acceptable performance standards for all students, assessing students with reasonable accommodations if necessary, and reporting schools' progress in meeting stated outcomes (Shriner, Ysseldyke, Thurlow, & Honetschlager, 1994).

Performance-based and other authentic assessment approaches are more compatible and supportive of children with and without disabilities than traditional standardized achievement testing. They also give a much broader picture of what students can actually do and of the necessary supports. And is that not what we truly want to know? As Nel Noddings has said, "We should move away from the question 'Has Johnny learned X?' to the far more pertinent question 'What has Johnny learned?'" (1992, p. 179).

Alternatives to traditional grading are available to school personnel who want distinctions on report cards and transcripts for students who have different goals or who receive modifications. The alternatives include pass/fail systems of grading, student self-assessments, contracts with students, criterion or checklist grading, and portfolios. Indeed, some teachers choose to use those alternative assessment methods for all students. Another alternative is to use the IEP as the vehicle for grade determination. Students with disabilities have an advantage over other students in that they have an IEP that, when used appropriately, clearly defines the objectives, any accommodations required during instruction and assessment, and the criteria or rubric for determining grades. Such clarification of expectations and success and of grading criteria would benefit any student.

The IEP is a powerful tool when working with school personnel reluctant to provide accommodations in instruction and assessment. The IEP is a federal requirement, and federal law supersedes state and local laws, policies, and practices that might allow accommodations identified in an IEP to be ignored. Perhaps the questions we should really be asking are, "What student wouldn't benefit from differentiation in assessment based on his or her learning style, MI strengths, or differing interests?" or "If we accommodated for everyone and used a portfolio approach in which students' actual performances and products are presented, what would be the purpose of grading and report cards?" By asking those questions, are we discussing whether students who are provided accommodations should be given different grades, or are we focused on good teaching to facilitate every child's learning?

8. Isn't inclusion in direct opposition to the No Child Left Behind Act and the national attention to higher standards and outcomes for students? Teachers must prepare students to score well on tests. Won't the presence of children with disabilities negatively impact students' and the school's scores?

The inclusion of children with disabilities is not in opposition to the movement to improve outcomes for students or the basic tenets of the No Child Left Behind (NCLB) Act. On the contrary, both inclusive education and NCLB call for high standards and student performance as they try to foster conditions leading to better instruction and learning, equality of opportunity to learn, and excellence in all children's performance. The four foundational pillars of NCLB are intended to offer every child—particularly the neediest—a quality education. The four pillars are (1) accountability for results in education; (2) flexibility in the way states and communities can use educational funds; (3) use of research-proven instructional methods and materials; and (4) parental influence, information, and choice.

Unfortunately, establishing standards and assessing account-ability for results through testing alone have not equalized learning opportunity or significantly altered student outcomes. Why? Kenneth Howe (1994) offers the following explanation:

> It strains credulity to suggest that implementing national standards and assessments could be anywhere near as effective a means of improving educational opportunity [or student outcomes] as addressing the conditions of schooling and society directly. It is rather like suggesting that the way to end world hunger is to first develop more rigorous standards of nutrition and then provide physicians with more precise means of measuring ratios of muscle-to-fat. (p. 31)

This said, what is promising about NCLB is the additional emphasis on highly qualified teachers, as well as flexibility in using effective, research-based curricular and instructional practices. In large part, these research-based practices are the very practices described in this book (in Chapters 5 and 6) that are supportive of inclusive education and that allow children with and without disabilities to thrive. Furthermore, NCLB's absolute emphasis on developing all students' literacy skills is important for students with disabilities because literacy is the gateway skill for access to the rest of the general education curriculum, which is a stated goal of the 1997 reauthorization of IDEA.

No evidence validates the concern that the presence of children with disabilities will negatively impact the district's norm- referenced achievement scores. In fact, studies have consistently indicated the contrary (see "Efficacy Data," p. 46–47). When students with disabilities are provided with supports and services to access the general education curriculum, their peers maintain state benchmark–level performances, and the students with disabilities experience higher academic and social achievement.

The inclusion of students with disabilities in general education, combined with the research-based curricula and instructional practices promoted by NCLB, should actually help teachers in standards-based classrooms. Students with (and without) disabilities need their teachers to learn and use the most effective teaching strategies, educational materials, and lesson formats currently known. It is possible for teachers to use standards as a curricular guide while retaining multilevel and student-centered instruction (Udvari-Solner, 1996). It is also possible for general and special educators to collaborate in planning and teaching (see "Preface," p. vi).

NCLB and the standards movement in no way are intended to standardize teachers' ways of teaching or students' ways of learning. Quite to the contrary, standards can be viewed as flexible, allowing different students in the same classroom to learn, practice, and show their accomplishments of a standard in different ways (Covington, 1996; Natriello, 1996; Reigeluth, 1997). For example, students may meet the mathematics standard, which means "explain to others how to solve a numerical problem," in different ways. Some students may use calculators or manipulatives to show understanding, others may be able to explain in a written paragraph, and still others may best express their knowledge by drawing diagrams or designing flow charts. In addition, students in the same classroom may be expected to focus on problems that range in complexity. Some students may describe the process for adding single or double digits while others may design and explain binomial equations.

9. How do we guarantee the safety (physical and emotional) of the other students when a student with emotional or behavioral disabilities is placed in general education classrooms?

It is not possible to guarantee that every classroom, hallway, playground, lunchroom, and bus is completely safe. Violence is a problem found in all aspects of U.S. society: homes, streets, restaurants, malls, and workplaces. An increasing number of children are perceived as troubled or troubling to their teachers, community, or family. More than 20 percent of U.S. children—the vast majority of whom are not eligible for special education—carry a weapon to high school every day. Clearly, violence is a societal problem and permanent solutions to student and societal violence will emerge only through community, interagency, and school collaboration. Yet solutions are emerging to make schools safer, more welcoming, and responsive to the needs of students considered behaviorally and emotionally challenging.

The most effective prevention of a student's rule-violating behavior includes effective instruction, personalized accommodations, and motivating learning experiences. We need to develop a constellation of resources and services for students experiencing behavioral or emotional challenges. That constellation includes, but is not limited to, (1) strategies for promoting and teaching responsibility; (2) social skills instruction; (3) teaching anger management and impulse control strategies to students; (4) strategies for involving, empowering, and supporting students; (5) strategies for involving, supporting, and empowering family members; (6) increasing collaboration among and personal support to students from the adults of the school; and (7) breaking with the traditional paradigm of schooling and what constitutes a student's day. (See Villa, Udis, & Thousand, 2002, for a detailed description.)

We can bring such a constellation of resources, supports, and services to the school setting and not send students away or immerse them in separate programs exclusively for children identified as emotionally or behaviorally challenging. In fact, it is often counterproductive to cluster students with emotional or behavioral issues in settings where they have limited access to prosocial models of behavior and where they are given the message that they do not belong with their peers (Kunc, 2002). Meeting the complex psychological and educational needs of students who are troubled or troubling is difficult. Matching intervention and support strategies to the child rather than sending a child away requires thoughtful consideration by teams of educators, parents, and students who care about and are committed to the child's survival and success in the community.

A basic responsibility of every school is to ensure freedom from physical harm for students and adults. No student has the right to harm another person. We know that students will sometimes place themselves and others in jeopardy. In anticipation, every school must have a well-articulated and well-understood crisis management system that promotes student responsibility and choice at each stage of a crisis. Choices may include (1) allowing a student to calm down in a predetermined setting; (2) allowing students, with parental permission, to leave school grounds for a time; (3) imposing in-school or out-of-school suspension for a short time until a team can convene and identify the next steps; (4) having a parent or mental health, social service, or police officer remove the student; or (5) allowing passive physical restraint by trained personnel. If a student is asked to leave school, he or she must have a safe and supervised place to go.

Social, emotional, and behavioral struggles in schools are not just issues faced by students with disabilities. Many students experience bullying in today's schools, including students who are racially, ethnically, and linguistically diverse; who dress or act outside the norms of the school; who have different body types; and who have learning differences. Educators are now asking new questions about the prevalence of teasing and bullying. Instead of asking, "Will George be teased if he is in a regular classroom?" they should ask, "How can we create school communities where all students feel safe, comfortable, and valuable?"

Schools must become communities where all students feel welcome and protected. If any student is scared or tormented at school, the student's placement should not be at risk. Instead, the school must change its practices and examine its culture. To prevent difficulties and promote safety, we should establish proactive conflict resolution strategies such as teaching students how to resolve their own conflicts through peer mediation, how to use anger management to defuse dangerous situations, and how to stop bullying. National movements such as teaching children to be peacemakers (Johnson & Johnson, 1995) or effective members of cooperative learning groups help students develop the skills they need to face controversy.

10. Inclusion would be nice but is unrealistic given increased student diversity, large class sizes, and decreased public funding. In some classes, 25 to 30 percent of students are identified as disabled. How can one teacher meet the needs of all students?

The reasons inclusion may be unrealistic have less to do with children and more to do with the way adults provide services. Given our cultural, racial, economic, and religious diversity, the idea that one educator working alone can successfully meet the widely diverse needs of all students seems outdated and impractical. A teacher working alone with traditional teaching methods (e.g., teacher-directed, predominantly independent or competitive student work structures; the same performance standard for all children) will be frustrated by student diversity.

A strikingly different organizational structure—a teaching team—is needed to meet heterogeneous needs. A teaching team involves two or more people who regularly distribute among themselves the planning, instructional, and evaluation responsibilities for the same students for an extended time. Teams can involve any combination of classroom teachers, specialized personnel, instructional assistants or paraprofessionals, student teachers, community volunteers, and students themselves. Inclusive education shifts the role from "lone arranger" to "partner with supports." A collaborative organizational structure takes advantage of the diverse experience, knowledge, and instructional approaches of various team members. In addition, the greater instructor-to-student ratio allows for more immediate and accurate diagnosis of student needs and for more active student learning.

Often the students themselves are overlooked as instructional and support resources. In inclusive classrooms, the teaching team invites students to partner in teaming arrangements (Thousand, Villa, & Nevin, 2002). Students function as instructors, as advocates for themselves and peers, and as decision makers serving on school governance committees to develop school curricula, inservice training programs, discipline policies, and organizational restructuring objectives.

11. Won't other children tease and ridicule children with disabilities?

Some children will probably be teased, but they may also do some teasing. An unfortunate reality is that children do face ridicule, teasing, and rejection in school. People are teased for many reasons (e.g., differences in perceived abilities, physical characteristics, ethnic background, religion, language, culture, socioeconomic status). Paradoxically, teasing can sometimes be a misguided attempt to express liking or attraction and to build personal connections. We do not believe that the solution to teasing is the removal of anyone who is different.

Adults cannot eliminate teasing and ridicule among children, but we can use strategies to reduce it. Teachers can promote a caring ethic within their classes through class meetings in which classmates determine ways to be more supportive of one another. Teachers may reduce teasing by teaching children the reasons for and the results of name-calling, teasing, and ridicule and by using learning structures that require and acknowledge positive treatment of classmates. For middle and high school students who have little to no experience with people with disabilities, activities to stir their concerns for social justice can be effective in building support for and minimizing teasing of students with disabilities. Having students plan for the transition and welcoming of a student with disabilities to their school can have positive effects.

At the heart of a solution to teasing is teacher and administrator modeling. Students observe, reflect on, and imitate adult behavior toward people who are different and the problem-solving strategies that adults use to deal with teasing and discrimination.

Experience leads us to believe that less ridicule occurs in inclusive schools—perhaps because of more explicit teaching of how to mediate conflict (see Johnson, Johnson, Dudley, & Burnett, 1992; Schrumpf & Jansen, 2002) and solve problems when teasing and discrimination occur. Children who begin their educational careers with children with disabilities seem comfortable with and accepting of difference.

12. Do proponents of inclusion advocate for eliminating special educators? How will children with disabilities have their unique needs met in a general education classroom without access to therapists and other trained personnel?

Inclusion proponents do *not* plan to eliminate special education teachers or other specialists such as psychologists, physical and occupational therapists, and social workers. Inclusionary environments *require* the participation of professionals who possess breadth and depth in many knowledge bases (e.g., human development and individual differences, particular reading or writing interventions, alternative communication strategies, mobility instruction, impulse control techniques).

The goal is always to ensure that every student receives needed supports and services. What is being called for is a change in the way some specialized personnel deliver expertise. Those who have worked alone and pulled children away from general education are being asked to work together to figure out how to address students' needs within general education classrooms. For specialists, that contextual change means being willing to become models, coaches, and members of coteaching teams to pass on the essential elements of their specialty to others (teachers, parents, volunteers, students). One result is a large number of people who can support and instruct a student throughout the day, thus increasing a student's access to valuable expertise and services that formerly only specialists provided. A second result is desegregation of both adults and students.

13. Some children need regular, intensive, individualized instruction to acquire specific skills. How can the needs of children with disabilities be met if we cannot take children out of general education classrooms for specific skill or functional life skill instruction?

The expectation in an inclusive school is that any student can and should receive focused and intensive instruction as needed. The instruction may occur in any location in the school that makes sense for the task, not in a special location that only students who are labeled or who get special help disappear to at times during the day or week. Who delivers the focused instruction depends on any number of variables, from professional expertise to interest or personal relationship with the child being instructed. Children, too, have proven to be exceptional at delivering focused instruction and should not be forgotten as instructional resources.

One element of meeting individualized learning needs requires changing the nature of the general education classroom. When children are grouped heterogeneously and allowed to progress at their own pace without regard to age, grade, or level of ability or disability, individualization naturally occurs. Specialized instruction should be available to any child who may wish or need it, but it should never be based on a label attached to a child. Schools that embrace a belief that learning can occur in many ways and in many different places have no trouble creatively designing ways to individualize for students. The false assumption exists that the only children who could benefit from functional life skill instruction are those eligible for special education. All children need functional life skills in a curriculum component.

14. If children with disabilities are never given the opportunity to interact with others like them, how will they develop an identity or recognize that there are other people with similar disabilities? Aren't we sending a message that it is not OK to associate with similar people because they should be with people who have no disabilities?

Inclusion is about the right to associate freely, not about denying children with disabilities the opportunity to know other people with similar disabilities or interests. The goal is to foster community, celebrate children's individual differences, and send the message that everyone has value. Allowing a child to go to the same school as his or her siblings and neighbors does not suggest that the child should or will not develop additional connections, relationships, and friendships outside the classroom with people who have similar interests and characteristics. Humans have a basic need to affiliate. In our society, we have created all types of affiliation organizations (e.g., Italian American associations, photography clubs) so people of common characteristics or interests can get together. Stainback, Stainback, and Sapon-Shevin (1994) and other leaders in multicultural education further stress the importance of developing positive self-identity for diverse groups of students within a school by supporting students' interest in affiliating with peers who have similar characteristics. The school bears the responsibility of creating planned opportunities for children with disabilities to get together to share experiences, if they wish. Like other school clubs, those opportunities could occur during or outside school hours. The key is to listen to the students, follow their lead, and help them organize affiliations with people whom they have identified. Choice is essential. Adults should not impose a particular identity group (e.g., students with Down syndrome) on children; only students know their affiliation interests and solidarity needs. Adults should not use a group's need for affiliation and solidarity as a rationale for segregation.

> 15. What can I do as one person? I do not have the systems-level support needed to make inclusion work.

In an address to the young people of South Africa on their Day of Affirmation in 1966, Robert Kennedy stated:

> Some believe there is nothing one man or one woman can do against the enormous array of the world's ills, against ignorance, injustice, misery, or suffering. Yet many of the world's greatest movements, of thought and action, have flowed from the work of a single person. A young monk began the Protestant Reformation, a young general extended an empire from Macedonia to the borders of the earth, and a young woman reclaimed the territory of France. It was the 32-year-old Thomas Jefferson who proclaimed that all humans are created equal.
>
> These people moved the world, and so can we all. Few will have the greatness to bend history itself, but each of us can work to change a small portion of events, and in the total of all of those acts will be written the history of this generation.
>
> It is from the numberless diverse acts of courage and belief that human history is shaped. Each time a person stands up for an ideal, or acts to improve the lot of others, or strikes out against injustice, [that person sends] forth a tiny ripple of hope, and crossing each other from a million different centers of energy and daring, those ripples build a current that can sweep

down the mightiest walls of oppression and resistance. (Cited in Schlesinger, 1978, p. 802)

What can one person do? First, believe that you *can* make a difference, even though the system is not yet behind you. Next, act in any and every way you can think of to increase the number of people and the depth of their conviction to promote inclusion. How do you do that?

- Know that there is strength in numbers. Build coalitions among disability rights groups, civil rights groups, parent groups, and other groups to embrace an inclusive philosophy.
- Create support groups of families and others like yourself to strategize how to get broader support.
- Locate or create a successful example of inclusion and showcase, share, and publicize it. Have people visit and talk with those involved with the effort.
- Get into positions of power. For example, run for the school board, become an officer of the teachers' union, or volunteer for committees that have influence in reforming policy or practice in your school.
- Model through your own actions the inclusion of adults and children with diverse interests and abilities in your professional and personal life. To create a change, become the change.
- Educate others about the ethical, legal, moral, and data-based rationale for inclusive education. Share with them the information from this book.
- Persevere and be compassionate. Remember that changing people's minds and beliefs takes time and causes emotional turmoil.
- Take action now.

References

Checkley, K. (1997). The first seven . . . and the eighth: A conversation with Howard Gardner. *Educational Leadership, 55*(1), 8–13.

Covington, M. V. (1996). The myth of intensification. *Educational Researcher, 25*(7), 24.

Crossley, R. (1997). *Speechless: Facilitating communication for people without voices.* New York: Dutton.

Gardner, H. (1983). *Frames of mind: The theory of multiple intelligences.* New York: Basic Books.

Gardner, H. (1993). *Multiple intelligences: The theory in practice.* New York: Basic Books.

Howe, K. (1994). Standards, assessment, and equality of educational opportunity. *Educational Researcher, 23*(8), 27–32.

Johnson, D., & Johnson, R. (1995). *Teaching students to be peacemakers* (3rd ed.). Edina, MN: Interaction Book Company.

Johnson, D., Johnson, R., Dudley, B., & Burnett, R. (1992). Teaching students to be peer mediators. *Educational Leadership, 50*(1), 10–13.

Kliewer, C., & Biklen, D. (2001). "School's not really a place for reading": A research synthesis of the literate lives of students with severe disabilities. *The Journal of the Association for Persons with Severe Handicaps, 26,* 1–12.

Kunc, N. (2002). Rediscovering the right to belong. In R. A. Villa & J. S. Thousand (Eds.), *Restructuring for caring and effective education: Piecing the puzzle together* (2nd ed., pp. 77–91). Baltimore: Paul H. Brookes.

Lilly, M. S. (1971). A training based model for special education *Exceptional Children, 37,* 745–749.

Natriello, G. (1996). Diverting attention from conditions in American schools. *Educational Researcher, 25*(8), 7–9.

Noddings, N. (1992). *The challenge to care in schools.* New York: Teachers College Press.

Reigeluth, C. M. (1997). Educational standards: To standardize or to customize learning? *Phi Delta Kappan, 79,* 202–206.

Schlesinger, A. M., Jr. (1978). *Robert Kennedy and his times.* New York: Ballantine Books.

Schrumpf, F., & Jansen, G. (2002). The role of students in resolving conflicts. In J. S. Thousand, R. A. Villa, & A. I. Nevin (Eds.), *Creativity and collaborative learning: The practical guide to empowering students, teachers, and families,* (2nd ed., pp. 283–302). Baltimore: Paul H. Brookes.

Shriner, J., Ysseldyke, J., Thurlow, M., & Honetschlager, D. (1994). "All means all"— Including students with disabilities. *Educational Leadership, 51*(6), 38–42.

Slavin, R. (1987). Ability grouping and achievement in elementary school: A best evidence synthesis. *Review of Educational Research, 57,* 293–336.

Stainback, S., Stainback, W., & Sapon-Shevin, M. (1994). A commentary on inclusion and the development of a positive self-identity by people with disabilities. *Exceptional Children, 60*(6), 486–490.

Thousand, J. S., Villa, R. A., & Nevin, A. I. (Eds.) (2002). *Creativity and collaborative learning: The practical guide for empowering students, teachers, and families* (2nd ed.). Baltimore: Paul H. Brookes.

Udvari-Solner, A. (1996). Examining teacher thinking: Constructing a process to design curricular adaptations. *Remedial and Special Education, 17,* 245–254.

Villa, R. A., & Thousand, J. S. (2000). *Restructuring for caring and effective education: Piecing the puzzle together* (2nd ed.). Baltimore: Paul H. Brookes.

Villa, R. A., Udis, J., & Thousand, J. S. (2002). Supporting students with troubling behavior. In J. S. Thousand, R. A. Villa, & A. I. Nevin (Eds.), *Creativity and collaborative learning: The practical guide to empowering students, teachers, and families* (2nd ed., pp. 135–156). Baltimore: Paul H. Brookes.

Chapter 8

Suggested Resources for Advancing Inclusive Education

Barbara E. Buswell, C. Beth Schaffner, Ann I. Nevin, and James W. Chapple

In spite of two decades of the inclusive education movement, many general and special educators have had limited exposure to alternative ways of educating students with disabilities other than in separate, special classrooms. Classroom teachers frequently hesitate to teach students with disabilities because they have not seen successful inclusive education in practice and do not know where to locate resource materials or people. In addition, many people are unaware that current school reform practices in general education offer instructional approaches that support successful inclusion of children and youths with disabilities.

How to Find Useful Materials

Resource materials are a critical element in ensuring the success of inclusive education. Many informative print resources are emerging, as are other media such as videotapes and compact discs, which demonstrate such supports. Because of the extensive number of resources available, educators and parents frequently state the difficulty of assessing which materials might be most useful. When selecting written resource materials, users must consider the audience and individuals' familiarity with the concept of inclusive education. For people just beginning to think about inclusion, resource materials should be brief, clear, and free of specialized terminology.

Materials should frame the big issues and describe strategies that support students. People using these materials should see the possibility of successfully including diverse students in neighborhood schools and general education classrooms. (See Chapter 3 for details about the big issues.)

How to Use Resources

People can use both print and audiovisual resources in many ways. When introducing inclusion in your school, district, or community, you can provide basic information in brief articles to select administrators, teachers, support people, school board members, and families. Parents report that they have made appointments with their neighborhood principals to watch a short video together. They then point out strategies from the video that could provide effective support for *their* child. Videos and slides are particularly useful when students with disabilities are shown participating with typical peers in general education activities.

The advent of Internet-accessible resources poses unique challenges and opportunities. The burgeoning number of Web sites related to disability issues should be evaluated. One source of evaluation criteria for Web-based learning resources is *MERLOT Teaching Well Online* at http://taste.merlot.org/eval.html. The researchers who maintain the site suggest three categories for evaluation: (1) quality of content, (2) potential effectiveness as a teaching and learning tool, and (3) ease of use. Esther Grassian (1998), a research librarian at the University of California, Los Angeles, provides a schema for critiquing discipline-specific Web sites. The schema is an important tool for ensuring that content-specific information about disability categories is accurate and up-to-date. The Web-based resources recommended in this chapter have been screened according to Grassian's standards.

Sources for Obtaining Inclusive Education Information

Many groups are currently emerging as good resources about inclusive educational strategies. Particular groups to consider contacting include the following: the Association for Supervision and Curriculum Development (ASCD), the National Association of State Boards of Education (NASBE), the National Education Association (NEA), the Association for Persons with Severe Handicaps (TASH), and other education or advocacy groups for specific categories of disabilities. In various states, people with expertise in supporting inclusive education can be contacted. They are affiliated with universities, private consultants, federally funded systems change projects, parent training and information centers, developmental disabilities planning councils, and state departments of education. Many states host yearly conferences and institutes that focus on strategies for successfully including all students.

This chapter identifies topical areas related to inclusion and suggests print and media resources to assist the reader in creating inclusive classrooms and school communities.

Annotated Bibliography

General Inclusion Resources

Books
Buswell, B. E., Schaffner, C. B., & Seyler, A. B. (1999). *Opening doors: Connecting students to curriculum, classmates, and learning.* Colorado Springs, CO: PEAK Parent Center.

Mastropieri, M. A., & Scruggs, T. E. (2000). *The inclusive classroom: Strategies for effective instruction.* Upper Saddle River, NJ: Prentice-Hall.

Salend, S. J. (2001). *Creating inclusive classrooms: Effective and reflective practices.* Upper Saddle River, NJ: Prentice-Hall.

Articles and Reports

Hines, R. (2001). *Inclusion in middle schools.* (Available from ERIC Clearinghouse on Elementary and Early Childhood Education, Children's Research Center, University of Illinois, 51 Gerty Dr., Champaign, IL 61820-7469.) ERIC Digest No. 459000.

Van der Klift, E., & Kunc, N. (2002). Beyond benevolence: Supporting genuine friendships in inclusive schools. In J. S. Thousand, R. A. Villa, & A. I. Nevin (Eds.), *Creativity and collaborative learning: The practical guide to empowering students, teachers, and families* (2nd ed., pp. 21–29). Baltimore: Paul H. Brookes.

Web-based Resources

Inclusion Web Site. Maintained by faculty in the Department of Special Education, University of Northern Iowa, Cedar Falls, Iowa, this site is designed for general education teachers, special education teachers, parents, and school staff members to help provide answers about accomplishing inclusive education. Resources for making accommodations are included, as well as links to other Web sites and resource lists for learning more about inclusive education. Available: http://www.uni.edu/coe/inclusion/index.html.

Renick, P. (Ed.). *Electronic Journal of Inclusive Education.* Retrieved December 29, 2002, from http://www.ed.wright.edu/~prenick.

Legal Resources

Laws and Court Decisions

Mills, G. E., & Duff-Mallams, K. (2000). Special education mediation. *Teaching Exceptional Children, 32*(4), 72–78.

Chandra Smith Consent Decree Web Site. This site provides up-to-date information on the progress of what has been called "the most sweeping case involving education since *Brown v. Board of Education.*" The site has links to the Consent Decree against the Los Angeles Unified School District, information about the committees that advise the Consent Decree administrators, and a schedule of activities that followed approval by U.S. District Court Judge Laughlin Waters in April 1995. Retrieved January 6, 2003, from http://www.cdlausd.com/.

Books

Heinz, W. (Ed.). (1999). *From education to work: Cross-national perspectives*. Boston: Cambridge University Press.

Articles and Reports

Straub, D., & Peck, C. (1994). What are the outcomes for non-disabled students? *Educational Leadership, 52*(4), 36–40.

Villa, R. A., Thousand, J. S., Nevin, A. I., & Meyers, H. W. (1996). The heterogeneous education teacher survey. *Exceptional Children, 63*(1), 45–53.

Web-based Resources

IDEA '97 Questions and Answers. Presented in a question-and-answer format, the resource is maintained by the U.S. Offices of Special Education and Rehabilitation Services. It has helpful resources for administrators, special and general education teachers, and families of people with disabilities. Available: http://www.ed.gov/policy/speced/leg/idea/q-and-a.html

School Reform and Inclusive Education

Books

Armstrong, T. (2000). *In their own way: Discovering and encouraging your child's multiple intelligences* (Rev. and updated ed.). New York: Putnam Publishing Group.

Glasser, W. (1998). *The quality school: Managing students without coercion* (3rd ed.). New York: HarperCollins.

Sapon-Shevin, M. (1998). *Because we can change the world: A practical guide to building cooperative inclusive classroom communities*. Needham Heights, MA: Allyn and Bacon.

Sizer, T. R. (1997). *Horace's compromise: The dilemma of the American high school* (Rev. ed.). Boston: Houghton Mifflin.

Villa, R. A., & Thousand, J. S. (2000). *Restructuring for caring and effective education: Piecing the puzzle together* (2nd ed.). Baltimore: Paul H. Brookes.

Wright-Johnson, R. (1994). *Toward inclusive classrooms*. West Haven, CT: National Education Association Professional Library.

Articles and Reports

Thousand, J. S., Nevin, A. I., Villa, R. A., & Quinn-Malgeri, C. (1996). Instilling collaboration for inclusive schooling as a way of doing business in public schools. *Remedial and Special Education, 17*(3), 162–181.

Strategies for Administrators

Books

Beninghof, A. M., & Singer, A. L. (1995). *Ideas for inclusion: The school administrator's guide*. Longmont, CO: Sporis West.

Skrtic, T. (2001). *Disability and democracy: Reconstructing (special) education for post-modernity*. New York: Columbia University, Teachers College Press.

VanDover, T. (1995). *The principal's guide to creating a building climate for inclusion*. Manhattan, KS: The Master Teacher.

Articles and Reports

Barnett, C., & Monda-Amaya, L. E. (1998). Principals' knowledge and attitudes toward inclusion. *Remedial and Special Education, 19*(3), 181–192.

Goor, M. B., Schwenn, J. O., & Boyer, L. (1997). Preparing principals for leadership in special education. *Intervention in School and Clinic, 32*(3), 133–141.

Praisner, C. (2003). Attitudes of elementary school principals toward the inclusion of students with disabilities. *Exceptional Children, 69*(2), 135–145.

Villa, R. A., & Thousand, J. S. (1992). How one district integrated special and general education. *Educational Leadership, 50*(2), 39–41.

Curriculum Adaptations and Teaching Strategies

Books

Artilles, A., & Ortiz, A. (2002). *English language learners with special education needs: Identification, assessment, and instruction*. Washington, DC: Center for Applied Linguistics.

Bigge, J., Best, S., & Heller, K. (2000). *Teaching individuals with physical, health, or multiple disabilities* (4th ed.). New York: Pearson Education.

Castagnera, E., Fisher, D., Rodifer, K., & Sax, C. (1998). *Deciding what to teach and how to teach it: Connecting students through curriculum and instruction.* Colorado Springs, CO: PEAK Parent Center.

Echevarria, J., & Graves, A. (1998). *Sheltered content instruction: Teaching English-language learners with diverse abilities.* Boston: Allyn and Bacon.

Fisher, D., Frey, N., & Sax, C. (1999). *Inclusive elementary schools: Recipes for success.* Colorado Springs, CO: PEAK Parent Center.

Nevin, A., & Hood, A. (2002). *Improving the Learning Outcomes of Preschool-Grade 12 Students with Disabilities Through Collaborative Action Research and Data Based Instruction.* (ERIC Document Reproduction Service No. ED467726)

Schoen, S. F., & Schoen, A. A. (2003). Action research in the classroom: Assisting a linguistically diverse learner with special needs. *Exceptional Children, 35*(3), 16–21.

Thousand, J. S., Villa, R. A., & Nevin, A. I. (Eds.) (2002). . *Creativity and collaborative learning: A practical guide to empowering students, teachers, and families* (2nd ed.). Baltimore: Paul H. Brookes.

Villa, R., Thousand, J., & Nevin, A. (2004). *A guide to co-teaching: Practical tips for facilitating student learning.* Thousand Oaks, CA: Corwin Press.

Wood, J. (2002). *Adapting instruction to accommodate students in inclusive settings* (4th ed.). Upper Saddle River, NJ: Merrill, Prentice-Hall.

Woodward, J., & Cuban, L. (2001). *Technology, curriculum, and professional development: Adapting schools to meet the needs of students with disabilities.* Thousand Oaks, CA: Corwin Press.

Articles and Reports

Johnson, D., & Johnson, R. (2000). Cooperative learning, values, and culturally plural classrooms. In M. Leicester, S. Modgill, & C. Modgill (Eds.), *Classroom issues: Practice, pedagogy, and curriculum* (Vol. 3, pp. 15–29). London: Falmer Press.

Nevin, A. I., Malian, I., & Williams, L. (2002). Self-determination and student-led Individual Education Programs: Special education teacher education candidates' perspectives. *Remedial and Special Education, 23*(2), 75–81.

Web-based Resources

Ferguson, D., Desjarlais, A., & Meyer, G. (2000, September). *Improving education: The promise of inclusive schooling.* National Institute for Urban Schools. Retrieved December 29, 2002, from http://www.edc.org/urban/lncbook.pdf.

Rose, D. (1999–2002). CAST Universal Design for Learning. 40 Harvard Mills Square #3, Wakefield, MA 01880-3233. Phone: 781-245-2212; e-mail: cast@cast.org. Available: http://www.cast.org.

Universal design: Ensuring access to general education curriculum. (1996). *Research Connections in Special Education, 5.* ERIC Clearinghouse No. EC 307411. Available: http://www.ericec.org.

Collaborative Teaming and Planning Processes

Books

Giangreco, M., Cloninger, C., & Iverson, V. (1997). *Choosing options and accommodations for children (COACH): A guide to planning inclusive education* (2nd ed.). Baltimore: Paul H. Brookes.

Idol, L., Nevin, A. I., & Paolucci-Whitcomb, P. (2000). *Collaborative consultation* (3rd. ed.). Austin, TX: Pro-Ed.

Wang, M., & Boyd, W. (2000). *Improving results for children and families: Linking collaborative services with school reform efforts.* New York: Information Age Publishing.

Articles and Reports

Falvey, M. A., Forest, M. S., Pearpoint, J., & Rosenberg, R. L. (2002). Building connections. In J. S. Thousand, R. A. Villa, & A. I. Nevin (Eds.), *Creativity and collaborative learning: A practical guide for empowering students, teachers, and families in an inclusive, multicultural, and pluralistic society* (2nd ed.), (pp. 29–54). Baltimore: Paul H. Brookes.

Giangreco, M. F., Cloninger, C. J., Dennis, R., & Edelman, S. (2002). Problem-solving methods to facilitate inclusive education. In J. S. Thousand, R. A. Villa, & A. I. Nevin (Eds.), *Creativity and collaborative learning: A practical guide for empowering students, teachers, and families* (2nd ed., pp. 111–134). Baltimore: Paul H. Brookes.

Harris, K., & Nevin, A. I. (1994). Bilingual special education teams. In L. Malave & J. Parla (Eds.), Annual Conference, *Journal of the National Association for Bilingual Education (pp. 25–36). Washington, DC: National Association for Bilingual Education.*

Nevin, A. I., Hood, A., & McNeil, M. (2002). Creating community in online (electronic) environments. In Helen Christensen (Ed.), *Re-educating the educator: Changing contexts and new challenges in teacher education* (pp. 127–151). New York: State University of New York Press.

Behavior Support Strategies

Books

Brendtro, L., Brokenleg, M., & Van Bockern, S. (1997). *Reclaiming youth at risk: Our hope for the future*. Bloomington, IN: National Educational Service.

Curwin, R., & Mendler, A. (1990). *Discipline with dignity*. New York: Pearson Education.

Articles and Reports

Schrumpf, F., & Jansen, G. (2002). The role of students in resolving conflicts. In J. S. Thousand, R. A. Villa, and A. I. Nevin (Eds.), *Creativity and collaborative learning: A practical guide to empowering students, teachers, and families* (2nd ed., pp. 283–302). Baltimore: Paul H. Brookes.

Villa, R. A., Thousand, J. S., & Udis, J. (2002). Supporting students with troubling behavior. In J. S. Thousand, R. A. Villa, & A. I. Nevin (Eds.), *Creativity and collaborative learning: A practical guide for empowering students, teachers, and families* (2nd ed., pp. 135–156). Baltimore: Paul H. Brookes.

Strategies for Promoting Belonging and Friendships

Books

Brannon, M. (1998). *Project SUCCESS: An inclusive service-learning curriculum for youth.* Washington, DC: United Cerebral Palsy, Corporation for National Service, and Learn and Serve America.

Katz, L., Sax, C., & Fisher, D. (1998). *Activities for a diverse classroom: Connecting students.* Colorado Springs, CO: PEAK Parent Center.

Articles and Reports

Van der Klift, E., & Kunc, N. (2002). Beyond benevolence: Supporting genuine friendships in inclusive schools. In J. S. Thousand, R. A. Villa, and A. I. Nevin (Eds.), *Creativity and collaborative learning: A practical guide for empowering students, teachers, and families.* (2nd ed., pp. 21–28). Baltimore: Paul H. Brookes.

Web-based Resources

National Institute for Urban School Improvement. (2000). *Improving education: The promise of inclusive schools.* Retrieved December 29, 2002, from http://www.edu.org/urban/Inclubook.htm.

Multimedia [all video]

Buswell, B. E., Schaffner, C. B., & Seyler, A. B. (1999). *An introductory workshop on friendship building strategies.* Includes workshop script, overhead transparencies, and handout originals. Colorado Springs, CO: PEAK Parent Center.

Seyler, A. B., & Schaffner, C. B. (2002). *An introductory workshop on tolerance: From bullying to belonging.* Includes workshop script, overhead transparencies, and handout originals. Colorado Springs, CO: PEAK Parent Center.

Individual Advocacy and Systems Change Strategies

Books

Seyler, A. B., & Buswell, B. E. (2001). *Individual education plans: Involved effective parents.* Colorado Springs, CO: PEAK Parent Center.

Web-based Resources

The Arc's Self-Advocacy Activities site is a well-researched, up-to-date resource maintained by the Arc, the organization formerly known as the National Association for Retarded Citizens. The site has links to a directory of self-advocacy groups, as well as a list of videos and other self-advocacy resources from other organizations. Available: http://thearc.org/misc/sadescr.html.

McGahey-Kovac, M. (2001). *A student's guide to the IEP.* Reston, VA: Council for Exceptional Children. Available (free) at the NICHCY Web site: http://www.nichcy.org/pubs/stuguide/st1.htm.

Differing Ability–Specific Information

Books

Nolan, C. (1987). *Under the eye of the clock: The life story of Christopher Nolan.* New York: St. Martin's Press.

Turnbull, A. P., Shank, M., Leal, D., Smith, S., & Turnbull, R. (2002). *Exceptional lives: Special education in today's schools* (3rd ed.). New York: Pearson Education.

Williams, Donna (1992). *Nobody, nowhere: The extraordinary autobiography of an autistic.* New York: Times Books.

Reports and Articles

Hood, A. T., & McNeil, M. (2002). Partner learning: The power source for students, schools and communities. In J. S. Thousand, R. A. Villa, & A. I. Nevin (Eds.), *Creativity and collaborative learning: The practical guide to empowering students, teachers, and families* (2nd ed., pp. 247–270). Baltimore: Paul H. Brookes.

Web-based Resources

Kluth, P. (1999, December). Developing successful schooling experiences for facilitative communication (FC) users: An interview with Franklin and Pat Wilson. *Facilitative Communication Institute Newsletter, 8*(1), 7–11. Available: http://soeweb.syr.edu/thefci/7-2klu.htm.

The National Information Center for Handicapped Children and Youth maintains up-to-date fact sheets for a wide range of disability categories. Available: http://www.nichcy.org.

Multimedia

Forest, M., Pearpoint, J., & Snow, J. (1994). *Inclusion*. [Motion picture]. Available from The Video Journal of Education, 5499 W. 3560 South, Salt Lake City, UT 84115-4225.

Godwin, T., & Wurzburg, G. (Producers). (1988). *Regular lives*. [Motion picture]. Available from PBS Home Video, P.O. Box 609, Melbourne, Fl, 32902.

Home Box Office (Producer). (1993). *Educating Peter*. [Motion picture]. Available from State of the Art, Inc., 4455 Connecticut Avenue, Suite B-200, Washington DC, 20008.

Joenro, Inc. (Producer). (1995). *The face of inclusion: A parent's perspective*. [Motion picture]. Syracuse, NY: Joenro, Inc., 111 Schuler St., Syracuse, NY 13203.

Lipsky, D.K., & Gartner, A. (1998). *Standards and inclusion: Can we have both?* [Motion picture]. Available from National Professional Resources, 25 S. Regent St., Port Chester, NY 10573; phone: 800-453-7461.

Moyer, J. (2000). *How big is your circle? A musical promoting healing of exclusion, ridicule and violence*. [Includes compact disc, script, and activity guide.] Cleveland, OH: Jeff Moyer Music, 670 Radford Dr., Cleveland, OH 44143-1905; phone: 216-442-2779.

Peytral Publications. (2002). *Collaborative planning: Transforming theory into practice*. Minnetonka, MN: Richard A. Villa, P.O. Box 1162, Minnetonka, MN 55345-0162; phone: 877-739-8725. Available: http://www.peytral.com

Peytral Publications. (2002). *Collaborative teaching: The co-teaching model*. Minnetonka, MN: Richard A. Villa, P.O. Box 1162; Minnetonka, MN 55345-0162; phone: 877-739-8725. Available: http://www.peytral.com.

Online Courses and Professional Development

Online Classes and Degree Programs for Students

Concord Consortium. The Concord Consortium is a nonprofit educational research and development organization based in Concord, Massachusetts. Available: http://www.Concord.org.

NovaNet®. NovaNet® is available 24 hours a day, seven days a week, and can be accessed either remotely or on site. NovaNet offers thousands of hours of instruction in more than 100 subject areas. The entire catalog of lessons is regularly updated, extended, and enhanced to respond to changes in technology, education and user needs. Available: http://www.pearsonedtech.com/novanet /features.htm.

Virtual High School. The Virtual High School is a nationwide collaboration of public and private high schools that offers 150 Internet-based courses to students in participating schools. Available: http://www.govhs.org/website.nsf.

Professional Development for Educators and Family Members

CEC Online Academy. Web-based seminars are available: http:// www.cec.sped.org/pd/webseminar/index.html. Web courses are available: http://www.cec.sped.org/pd/aoa.html. Self-study packets from previous CEC staff development options are available: http://www.cec.sped.org/pd/self_study_packets.html. To encourage practitioners to read professional journals, a joint service between the journal *TEACHING Exceptional Children* and the organization www.journalearning.com permits readers to complete a quiz about the content of the issue, then to fax or mail it (with a small fee). Readers are then issued 0.2 (two tenths) continuing education credits for professional development.

Epilogue

When you serve as a trailblazer in inclusive education, your learning is grounded in what you glean from others. We hope this chapter of current work, both printed and multimedia, will help you and others to make inclusive education successful. If our information has inspired you, be sure to let others know. Remember that in inclusive education, as in other areas, the past is shared through stories, and the future is built on dreams.

References

Grassian, E. (1998). Thinking critically about discipline-based World Wide Web resources. Retrieved January 6, 2003, from http://www.library.ucla.edu/libraries/college/help/critical/discipline.htm. Site maintained by UCLA library.

Index

About the Authors

Editors

Richard A. Villa has worked with thousands of teachers and administrators throughout North America and the world in developing and implementing instructional support systems for educating all students within general education settings. Rich has been a classroom teacher, special education coordinator, pupil personnel services director, and director of instructional services. He has authored more than 100 articles and book chapters regarding inclusive education and has co-edited seven books for teachers, administrators and parents (*Creating an Inclusive School; Restructuring for Caring and Effective Education: Piecing the Puzzle Together; Creativity and Collaborative Learning: A Practical Guide for Empowering Students and Teachers,* and *A Guide to Co-Teaching: Practical Tips for Facilitating Student Learning*). Rich has presented at numerous national and international conferences and is known for his enthusiastic, humorous style of presenting.

Richard A. Villa, President, Bayridge Consortium, Inc., 113 West "G" St., Suite 444, San Diego, CA 92101. Phone: 619-795-3602. E-mail: ravillabayridge@cs.com. Website: http://www.ravillabayridge.com.

Jacqueline S. Thousand is a professor in the College of Education at Cal State San Marcos where she coordinates the College of Education's special education credential and masters programs. She is a well-known author, systems change consultant, and disability rights advocate. She has authored numerous books, research articles, and chapters on issues related to organizational change strategies, universal design and differentiated instruction, collaborative teaming processes, cooperative learning, creative problem solving, student self-determination, and discipline with dignity. Her service includes journal editorial board membership and international teacher development through partnerships with teacher trainers in a number of countries including Italy, Honduras, the Netherlands, Norway, and the Czech Republic.

Jacqueline S. Thousand, Cal State San Marcos, San Marcos, CA. Phone: 760-750-4022. E-mail: jthousan@csusm.edu.

Contributors

Barbara E. Buswell, Executive Director, PEAK Parent Center, Inc., 611 North Weber, Suite 200, Colorado Springs, CO 80903. Phone: 719-531-9400.

James W. Chapple, Professional Instructor, Ashland University, 108 University Center, Elyria, OH 44035. Phone: 440-366-7508. E-mail: Chappjw@aol.com.

Mary A. Falvey, Ph.D., Professor, Division of Special Education, California State University–Los Angeles, 5151 State University Dr., Los Angeles, CA 90032. Phone: 323-343-4406. Fax: 343-343-5605.

Douglas Fisher, Professor, School of Teacher Education, San Diego State University, 4283 El Cajon Blvd., #100, San Diego, CA 92105. E-mail: dfisher@mail.sdsu.edu.

Nancy Frey, Assistant Professor, School of Teacher Education, San Diego State University, 5500 Campanile Dr., San Diego, CA 92182. E-mail: nfrey@mail.sdsu.edu.

Katharine Shepherd Furney, Assistant Professor, Department of Education, University of Vermont, 449A Waterman Building, Burlington, VT 05405-0160. Phone: 802-656-1348. Fax: 802-656-2702. E-mail: Katharine.Furney@uvm.edu.

Christine C. Givner, Professor, Division of Special Education, California State University–Los Angeles, 5151 State University Dr., Los Angeles, CA 90032. Phone: 323-343-4402. Fax: 323-343-5605.

Joanne Godek, Consulting Teacher, Orchard School, 2 Baldwin Ave., South Burlington, VT 05465.

Denyse Patel Henry, consultant for an educational software company. E-mail: denyse_henry@yahoo.com.

M. G. (Peggy) Kelly, Professor and Associate Dean, College of Education, California State University San Marcos, 333 S. Twin Oaks

Valley Rd., San Marcos, CA 93096-0001. Phone: 760-750-4315. Fax: 760-750-4323. E-mail: pkelly@csusm.edu.

Paula Kluth, Independent Scholar and Education Consultant & Adjunct Professor of Education, National-Louis University, 4539 N. Lowell Ave., Chicago, IL 60630. E-mail: pkluth@earthlink.net.

Norman Kunc, Axis Consulting, 335A Machaleary St., Nanimo, British Columbia, V9R 3G9, Canada. Phone: 250-754-8508. E-mail: axis@island.net.

Ann I. Nevin, Professor Emerita, Arizona State University, and Visiting Professor at Florida International University. Phone: 954-885-7662. E-mail: DrAnnNevin@bellsouth.net.

Alice Quiocho, Associate Professor, Language and Literacy, College of Education, Uh 327, Cal State San Marcos, San Marcos, CA 92096-0001. Phone: 760-750-4035. Fax: 760-750-3237. E-mail: aquiocho@csusm.edu.

Mary Lynn Riggs, Principal, St. Albans City School, 29 Bellows St., St. Albans, VT 05478. Phone: 802-527-0565. E-mail: csprin@sover.net.

C. Beth Schaffner, Coordinator of Inclusive Schooling, PEAK Parent Center, Inc., 6055 Lehman Dr., Colorado Springs, CO 80918. Phone: 719-531-9400.

Julie Smith, Assistant Professor, Special Education, University of Hawaii–Manoa. E-mail: juliesmi@hawaii.edu.

Susan Bray Stainback, Professor Emerita, University of Northern Iowa. E-mail: sbrays@alltel.net.

Deborah Tweit-Hull, San Diego, CA. E-mail: tweithul@cox.net.

Jonathan Udis, Upstream Educational Services, 46 East Hill, Middlesex, VT 05602. Phone: 802-229-4616. E-mail: jonudis@together.net.

Alice Udvari-Solner, University of Wisconsin–Madison, Department of Curriculum and Instruction, 225 N. Mills St., Madison, WI 53706. E-mail: alice@education.wisc.edu.

Emma Van der Klift, Axis Consulting, 335A Machaleary St., Nanimo, British Columbia, V9R 3G9, Canada. Phone: 250-754-8508. E-mail: axis@island.net.

Joe Vargo, 241 Dorchester Avenue, Syracuse, NY, 13203. Phone: 315-463-2290.

Rosalind Vargo, 241 Dorchester Avenue, Syracuse, NY, 13203. Phone: 315-463-2290.

Related ASCD Resources: Inclusion

At the time of publication, the following ASCD resources were available; for the most up-to-date information about ASCD resources, go to http://www.ascd.org. ASCD stock numbers are noted in parentheses.

Multimedia

Learning Styles Professional Inquiry Kit (eight activity folders and a videotape), Pat Burke Guild, Kathi Hand (#998213)

Online Courses

Differentiating Instruction

Print Products

Classroom Leadership, November 2003: Teaching All Students (#103392)
Curriculum Update, Spring 2003: Targeted Attention, Special Rewards (#103042)
Inclusive Schools in Action: Making Differences Ordinary, James McCleskey, Nancy Waldron (#100210)

Videotapes

Inclusion (three tapes) (#495044)
The Lesson Collection Tape 6 Punctuation (Middle School) (#499263)

For more information, visit us on the World Wide Web (http://www.ascd.org), send an e-mail message to member@ascd.org, call the ASCD Service Center (800-933-ASCD or 703-578-9600, then press 2), send a fax to 703-575-5400, or write to Information Services, ASCD, 1703 N. Beauregard St., Alexandria, VA 22311-1714 USA.